Silver Boxes

OTHER BOOKS BY FLORENCE LITTAUER

After Every Wedding Comes a Marriage
The Best of Florence Littauer
Blow Away the Black Clouds
How to Get Along with Difficult People
It Takes So Little to Be Above Average
Hope for Hurting Women
Looking for God in All the Right Places
Out of the Cabbage Patch
Personalities in Power
Personality Plus
The Pursuit of Happiness
Raising the Curtain on Raising Children
Say It with CLASS
Shades of Beauty (co-authored with Marita Littauer)
Your Personality Tree

Florence Littauer

Silver Boxes

The Gift of Encouragement

THOMAS NELSON
Since 1798

SILVER BOXES

Unless otherwise noted, all scripture quotations are from the authorized King James Version. Other scripture quotations are from the following sources: The Amplified Bible (AMP). Copyright © 1965 Zondervan Publishing House. *The Living Bible* (TLB), copyright 1971 by Tyndale House Publishers, Wheaton, IL. Used by permission. *The Good News Bible*, Today's English Version (TEV); Old Testament: Copyright © American Bible Society 1976; New Testament: Copyright © American Bible Society 1966, 1971, 1976. The Holy Bible, New International Version (NIV). Copyright © 1973, 1978, 1984 International Bible Society. Used by permission of Zondervan Bible Publishers. The New King James Bible (NKJV), New Testament, copyright © 1979 by Thomas Nelson, Inc., Publishers. The Revised Standard Version of the Bible (RSV), copyrighted 1946, 1952, © 1971, 1973 by the Division of Christian Education of the National Council of Churches of Christ in the U.S.A., used by permission. The New American Standard Bible (NASB), © 1960, 1962, 1963, 1968, 1971, 1972, 1973, 1975, 1977 by The Lockman Foundation. Used by permission.

For the convenience of those who want to know more about the Personality Profile mentioned in this book, a copy of the profile and scoring sheets have been provided on pages 151–154.

Library of Congress Cataloging-in-Publication Data

Littauer, Florence, 1928–
    Silver boxes : the gift of encouragement / Florence Littauer.
        p.   cm.
    ISBN 978-0-7852-9732-1
    1. Encouragement—Religious aspects—Christianity.   I. Title.
BV4647.E53L57   1989
241'.672—dc20   89-30432
                                                                                    CIP

    4 5 6 7 8 9 LBM 20 19

Printed in the United States of America

*When you've given your best,
you can keep the rest.*

**Numbers 18:30,
author's paraphrase**

SILVER BOXES

My words were harsh and hasty
And they came without a thought.
Then I saw the pain and anguish
That my bitter words had brought.

Bitter words that I had spoken
Made me think back through the past;
Of how many times I'd uttered
Biting words whose pain would last.

Then I wondered of the people
I had hurt by things I'd said;
All the ones I had discouraged
When I didn't use my head.

Then I thought about my own life,
Of painful words I've heard;
And of the times I'd been discouraged
By a sharp and cruel word.

And now clearly I remember
All the things I might have done;
But, by a word I was discouraged
And they never were begun.

Lord, help my words be silver boxes,
Neatly wrapped up with a bow;
That I give to all so freely,
As through each day I gladly go.

Silver boxes full of treasure,
Precious gifts from God above;
That all the people I encounter
Might have a box of God's own love.

Michael Bright
1989

Contents

	Introduction	ix
1	LITTLE SILVER BOXES WITH BOWS ON TOP	1
2	A SILVER BOX IN EVERY ROOM	5
3	TOY BOXES	11
4	GIFT BOXES	18
5	SECRET BOXES	27
6	MAILBOXES	39
7	FLOWER BOXES	51
8	SCHOOL BOXES	62
9	STOLEN BOXES	68
10	SPECIAL BOXES	84
11	A BOX OF PEACE	91
12	SAFE-DEPOSIT BOXES	97
13	RECEIVING SILVER BOXES	109
14	BOXES OF BROKEN DREAMS	122
15	MUSIC BOXES	136
	Notes	149
	Personality Profile	151
	Pesonality Scoring Sheet	153

Introduction

Is It Edifying?

As Fred and I were raising our family, we liked to memorize verses that were practical in everyday life. One that we used frequently to set the tone for our dinner time conversation was Ephesians 4:29, "Let no corrupt communication proceed out of your mouth, but that which is good to the use of edifying, that it may minister grace unto the hearers."

Whatever we said had to meet the test of Ephesians 4:29. Our words were to be positive, not negative. They were to build up the family members, and they were to do a favor for the recipient. As we discussed this verse and practiced using it in personal application, we condensed it to three little words, "Is it edifying?"

Fred and I agreed with the children that they were allowed to ask us the same question. If one of us came out with a sarcastic or negative comment, one of them could ask, "Is it edifying?" We then had to agree that what we had said was not good to the use of edifying and did not do a favor to the listeners.

I once heard Freddie explaining to a little friend, "If she asks you 'Is it edifying?' that means you've said something bad. The best way to get out of trouble is to say you're sorry and watch what comes out of your mouth from then on."

He had learned his lesson well.

This book is based on Ephesians 4:29, and it is my hope that it will help all of us to eliminate negative words from our vocabulary and to say instead those things that will build others up and give a present to those who are listening.

"Don't use bad language. Say only what is good and helpful to those you are talking to, and what will give them a blessing" (Ephesians 4:29, TLB).

"You must stop letting any bad word pass your lips, but only words that are good for building up as the occasion demands, so that they will result in spiritual blessing to the hearers" (Ephesians 4:29, WILLIAMS).

"Don't say anything bad but only what is good, so that you help where there's a need and benefit those who hear it" (Ephesians 4:29, BECK).

Silver Boxes

Little Silver Boxes with Bows on Top

*I*t was a typical old New England style church with a long red-carpeted center aisle and high-arched, stained-glass windows depicting Moses delivering the Ten Commandments. It was the kind of church where people came early to get the back seats, somehow afraid that sitting up front would make them too spiritual or put them within eye-contact range of the pastor. It was the staff of this traditional church that had called me to come and teach them how to give better talks and how to awaken the hearts of their lethargic flock.

It was a Sunday morning in that church. I had come a day ahead to observe the church service and get a feel for the people and their needs. As I sat relaxed and grateful that I had one Sunday when I wasn't scheduled to speak, I heard the pastor say, "I see that Florence Littauer is in our congregation this morning, and I think it would be nice if she came up and gave us a few words." Never at a loss for words, I stirred in my seat. As I started to rise, the pastor added, "In fact, why don't we have Mrs. Littauer give the children's sermon."

I had never given a children's sermon, and I thought to myself, *There's a big difference between saying a few words and delivering a children's sermon.* I wanted to reply, "I don't do children's sermons," but I realized that since I was there to teach the staff how to speak spontaneously, I could hardly refuse the invitation. As I walked up the aisle, the pastor asked all the children to come forward and out of each pew darted little ones following me like an instant Pied Piper.

What was I going to say? I couldn't fail or my credibility would be lost. I sent up a "Lord help me" prayer and instantly Ephesians 4:29 came to my mind. It was the verse Fred and I had taught our children so that they would speak kindly to one another. By this time the little ones from ages three to twelve were filing into the empty front rows, and I turned to stand before them.

"This morning I'm going to teach you one verse that I taught my children. Do you think you could learn one verse?" They all nodded happily, and I was pleased that they were so responsive.

"Whenever we study a verse, we want to ask ourselves three things: what does it say, what does it mean, and how does it apply to me today?"

I then stated the verse: "Let no corrupt communication proceed out of your mouth, but that which is good to the use of edifying, that it may minister grace unto the hearers" (Ephesians 4:29).

When I asked if anyone knew what that verse meant, they all shook their heads. Those big words were too much for them. "Let's take it apart," I suggested. "What is communication?" They gave quick answers: talking, saying words.

"What is corrupt communication?"

A boy of about ten replied with a twinkle, "Bad words."

"That's right," I said, "God does not want us to let any bad words come out of our mouth. What does he want us to say? Words that are good and that will edify. What does it mean to edify?"

Deep looks came over their faces as they wondered what it meant to edify. One girl spoke up. "Does it mean to build up?"

I was thrilled that she had come up with the right answer.

"That's perfect," I said enthusiastically. "We are not to say bad words but good words that will build each other up. Now what does it mean to *minister grace?*"

We discussed the fact that to *minister* is to serve and give to others. One of the older children spoke up and said, "We learned in Sunday school that grace is God's unmerited favor." The others looked at her as if she were speaking a foreign language, but I congratulated her and amplified her statement. "That's great. Grace is a gift we didn't necessarily deserve."

I then went on to explain that Paul wrote this verse to the church in Ephesus because he had heard that the nice people were saying unkind things about each other. Even though they were good Christians, they were saying bad words, and he had to give them some advice about what should come out of their mouths. He had to tell these well-meaning people to stop dropping bad words on each other and start giving out messages that would build each other up and do others a favor.

"Is it possible," I asked, "that some of the good families in *this* church occasionally say things to each other that are not kind?"

The eyes of these little ones grew big and some even nodded yes, it was possible.

"Let's see now how this one verse applies to you and me. We've taken it apart to find out what it really teaches; we've seen what it meant to those ancient people in Ephesus; now what does it say to us good church-going people seated here today? What kind of corrupt communication or bad words are we apt to let out of our mouths?"

"Swearing. Vulgar language. Gossip. Talking down to others. Saying nasty words to your mother."

They all gasped on this last one, and we all agreed that saying nasty words to your mother was definitely corrupt communication.

"How can we make our words good to the use of edifying?" I asked.

They gave an assortment of answers. "Say nice things to others. Give out compliments. Be cheerful. Help our parents when they're cranky. Tell the truth." As we reviewed the process of building each other up, one bright boy spoke up, "Our words should be like building blocks."

I was delighted with this simple, clear picture, "That's a great idea. We should think of each word as a block, and we should keep adding good words to each other's pile of blocks until the pile gets higher and higher."

As I was demonstrating with my hands putting one block on top of another on this imaginary pile, a little boy called out, "And we shouldn't go around and knock other people's blocks down!"

They all giggled, and I latched onto his brilliant comparison. "What a great thought you've come up with! What a perfect picture! Here's a whole pile of good words, and then someone comes along with a negative remark and it knocks all the blocks down."

They got the message clearly, and I was delighted with this little group's enthusiasm and participation. They were more responsive and eager than many adult audiences, and I began to wonder why I hadn't done children's sermons before. I then moved on to the last part of the verse that says our words should minister grace—do a favor, give a present to each other. I explained that when our words come out of our mouths, they should be like little presents all wrapped up to be given away. The idea of presents brightened them all up, and then one precious little girl stood up, stepped into the aisle, and said loudly to the whole congregation, as if serving as my interpreter, "What she means is that our words should be like little silver boxes with bows on top."

As the adults nodded and murmured affirmations, I exclaimed, "What a beautiful thought! Our words should be gifts to each other, little silver boxes with bows on top."

What more could I say? The children had taught the verse to each other and to me in a way none of us could easily forget. We were not to say any bad, vulgar, unkind words. But we were to think of each word as a building block, one on top of another, ever reaching higher and higher. And we were never to go around knocking other people's blocks down. We were to make sure our words were like little silver boxes with bows on top—verbal presents that would encourage others.

When a lesson is taught by the children, it is clear enough even for adults to understand and remember.

Little did I know at that time what that child's contribution would become: first a message, and now a book full of *silver boxes*.

"Out of the mouth of babes and sucklings hast thou ordained strength" (Psalm 8:2).

A Silver Box in Every Room

Although I've never been asked to give a children's sermon again, I could never forget that little girl's words, "What she means is our words should be like little silver boxes with bows on top."

In November of 1987, I spoke at the evening service of Calvary Church in Winter Park, Florida. I built my message around Ephesians 4:29 and used the silver box example. I couldn't help noticing how closely the children and teens were listening. One boy about twelve said to me afterwards, "You were so interesting that I never even opened the book I brought to read." I was so glad!

The following night as I arrived at the same church to do a Personality Plus Seminar, a lady came up to me with a little mirrored silver box with a bow on top. It was a Christmas tree ornament she had seen in a store. She handed it to me and said, "I was in a Christmas store today, and when I saw this little silver box with a bow on top, I just had to buy it for you. Put it on your tree, and every time you pass by you'll be reminded to say kind words—little silver boxes with bows on top."

The little box never made it to a tree, but I've carried it with me ever since. When I open my briefcase and see the silver box in the corner, I'm reminded to give out words that will edify and do a favor to the hearer.

That same night, a dynamic-looking lady came striding toward me with a gift box wrapped in silver paper. She started off by thanking me for the previous night's message, and then she added, "You made me realize that I haven't said a kind word to my husband in years." Her teenage daughter standing behind her was amazed at her mother's frankness.

She looked over her mother's shoulder and nodded to me that her mother's comment was correct.

The mother then continued, "And I haven't said much nice to my children, either." The daughter's eyes became even bigger as she heard her mother's words of true confession. "So this afternoon I went out in the garage and dusted off some old empty Christmas boxes. I went downtown and bought a roll of silver paper and a bag of silver bows. I wrapped up the empty boxes and made them into silver boxes with bows on top. I have put one in every room in the house so that no matter where I look I'll see a silver box with a bow on top and be reminded to say nice words to those around me." The daughter gave me a "that'll be the day" look, and the mother handed me a silver box. "This one's for you to keep."

I brought her silver box home, and it still sits on Fred's desk in our office to remind us all to say kind words. Often visitors ask if it's someone's birthday, and we have an opportunity to explain that our words should be like little silver boxes with bows on top.

I was asked to give the silver box message for a couples' banquet in Wichita, Kansas. The committee wrapped up hundreds of gift boxes in silver paper and decorated the long banquet tables with shiny piles of these boxes. The ladies had spent hours wrapping the boxes, but they felt it was worth the trouble to tie into my theme so appropriately. Plus, they were going to get double use of the silver boxes by collecting them afterwards and decorating the tables the next month for the Christmas banquet. They were thrilled with how beautiful the boxes looked and with how easy it would be next month when they had only to add a little greenery to what would become Christmas presents.

The audience became so involved in the message that when I'd pick up a little box and say, "Our words should be like a little silver box with a bow on top," they'd mouth the words along with me.

As I was finishing my message, I noticed the committee ladies lined up along the edge of the large gymnasium, holding empty black trash bags. It passed through my mind that I'd never seen women so eager to gather trash that they would be standing at the alert ready to move en masse at the sound of the pastor's closing amen. I finished and he prayed. As the men and women moved toward the back of the room, the trash ladies advanced with their bags. I soon learned that they were planning to gather up the silver boxes to save for the next month, but as they rushed in, they found the tables empty. All the people had taken home a sample box to place in a spot where they could be reminded that their words should be like little silver boxes with bows on top.

At one church where I did "Silver Boxes" as a luncheon message, the committee wrapped up tiny silver boxes for each person to take home as a favor. Inside each box was a little slip of paper. They had typeset Ephesians 4:29 and added a brief message. "May each word we say be as a little silver box with a bow on top."

Each lady left holding her little silver box and vowing to keep it in a visible place forever.

Another group had cut a mirror into little squares. They glued a bow onto the front of each square and wrote Ephesians 4:29 beneath it. On the back of each silver box with a bow on top, they attached a little magnet disk so the box would fasten onto the refrigerator and be visible constantly as a reminder.

As the silver-box message has become popular, I have added more little boxes to my collection. Now when I speak, I have a pile of silver boxes and pick up different ones to hold and use as I go along. I have a tiny sterling silver pill box, several Christmas tree ornaments, and some larger boxes— all of which were given to me by people who loved the concept and wanted to contribute.

Before Christmas in 1988, while Fred and I were in New York shopping, we saw a black sweater I am wearing in the picture on the back cover of this book. It was on a mannequin, and when we saw the sequined silver bow splashed across the front, we knew it had been created just for me.

After Christmas when I was perusing a rack of marked-down holiday shoes, I was stunned to see a smashing pair of silver shoes each with a large bow on the side. I reached for them wondering what size they were and how expensive. They were my size and they fit perfectly, but there was no price marked.

Since this was a fancy boutique, I hardly dared to ask.

When the saleslady found the box, she showed me the original price of $200. My heart gave up as I assumed the most they could possibly be marked down to would be $100. But as the lady looked the box over, she said, "I can't believe this. They've cut this price to $29.95." I grabbed the shoes quickly before she could change her mind, and I have loved wearing them when I speak on silver boxes with bows on top.

Marte Simpson dropped me a note on how her fourth-grade teacher had encouraged her to pursue photography. At the bottom she wrote:

"P. S. I love your silver bow suit and your silver shoes. How special God is to give you a special silver box garment. It's perfect!"

Although I put my silver box outfit together for fun, I have found that it helps people retain the message. Every visual illustration people can hold in their minds sustains the value of the inspiration.

My friend Dee Dee wrote that she had received silver boxes as she was growing up, but because of some marriage difficulties, she has not been saying kind words for years.

I am now realizing since listening to you that silver boxes have not been coming out of my mouth—or his—since our problems began. My eight-year-old daughter's self-esteem is zero. She is trying to do the best she can so people will give her silver boxes. I had heard you speak last year, but today your words finally sank in. I need to have silver boxes everywhere around me at all times—car, house, and camper. Thank you for sharing your silver boxes. I will keep the picture of you with the silver-glitter bow on your outfit and remember your message. Silver boxes with bows need to be in my life now and forever.

At the Southern California Women's Retreat, teenager Cherie Simpson came up and presented me with a tiny silver box. It was made out of silver paper folded to become a box. Cherie showed me how she made this box using the Japanese paper-folding art of origami. I was fascinated at how quickly she could create a little silver box and asked if she could find the instructions and send them to me so I could include them in this book.

When I received a package from her, it included three little silver boxes, a package of silver origami paper, and the instructions at the end of this chapter. Cherie also enclosed her KIDS' ART GALLERY "business card." With her parents' encouragement, when she was ten years old, Cherie set up shop in Northridge, California, where she teaches others how to develop their artistic talent—and, now, how to give silver boxes.

If you can't find the silver origami paper, it may be ordered from: Yasutomo, Brisbane, CA 94005.

Dorothy McKendry wrote, "Thank you a million times for all you have given me this weekend. This poem is simple and short, but as I was watching Florence on stage with that beautiful Christmas tree behind her and listened to her words, I just felt a compulsion to write this simple poem for you:

> Christmas comes but once a year,
> With its jingle bells and its flying reindeer.
> But our friendships are with us all year long,
>   Growing deep, growing strong.
> So as Christmas presents sparkle gold,
>   Here's a *Silver Box*, for you to hold.

"Reckless words pierce like a sword, but the tongue of the wise brings healing" (Proverbs 12:18, NIV).

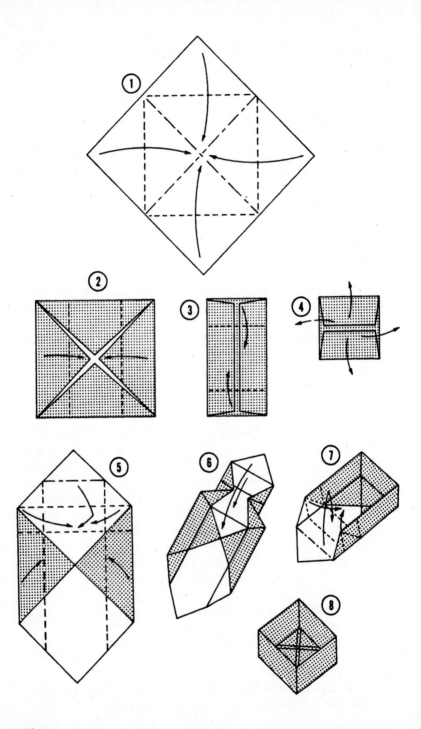

3

Toy Boxes

As children love the toy boxes full of games, dolls, and trucks, so they seem to enjoy and understand the silver boxes full of encouraging words.

After I presented the silver box message at Calvary Church, a boy came up to me and handed me a note written on lined notebook paper.

> Florence
>
>> God bless you!
>> I love you!
>> You really touched me!
>> I'll watch what I say!
>
> 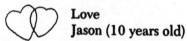 Love
> Jason (10 years old)

I keep Jason's letter with me, and when I speak, I use it as an example of how children will respond when they can understand the message and feel the speaker really cares for them. After telling about Jason one night, I received a note from the hand of a little seven-year-old.

As I leaned down to hear him, he whispered, "My name is Jason, too, and I wanted to give you a note so you could talk about me, too."

His words were written on a jagged piece of notebook paper ripped off the bottom of a page, but he handed it to me as proudly as if it were on gold foil. One side had hearts on it and said, "I love you from Jason." The other side had a house with many windows and a sketch of Jason standing on top of a box, which I assume represented the silver box with a bow on top. Perhaps he was to be the bow. His self-portrait had a triangle for a body with a big heart filling the space in the center. I was touched that he, at seven years old, had listened, understood, and responded.

A little girl named Angie gave me a page that said,

Florence Littauer, I love you and your message. I was really touched and thanks for your silver boxes.

 Love, Angie

She had drawn a large silver box on the bottom of the page, and she pointed to it saying, "This is my silver box with a bow on top for you."

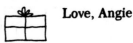

One night after a church service a little boy with big bright eyes came up to me and said, "I want your little box to take home." The box he pointed to was one of the special ones that had been given to me, and I had used it to illustrate my message.

"You want my silver box?" I asked.

"Yes, I need to have it."

"I'm so sorry," I replied, "but I need to keep it with me to use when I give this message."

Tears came to his eyes and he said, "I really need your box."

"What would you do with it?"

"I'd put it on my dresser and look at it every day so I'd say nice words."

Suddenly I realized it was more important for him to have the box than for me to keep it. I remembered the verse, "To him that knoweth to do good, and doeth it not, to him it is sin" (James 4:17).

As I leaned down and placed the box in his hand, he

reached up, kissed me, and whispered, "I'll always remember you."

Later I thought of the possible consequences if I had refused to give him my silver box. He could have gone away thinking, *She talks about giving out silver boxes, but she wouldn't give one to me.* He could have decided, *All adults are selfish. All speakers are phonies.*

I don't know what that wistful little boy did with the box. Perhaps he'll keep it on his dresser for years and teach the lesson to his friends. Perhaps his mother will throw it away one day when she's on a cleaning binge. No matter what happens, I know what I did was right, and maybe it will make a difference in that child's life.

A ten-year-old girl wrote me a note on one of the cards that had been placed in the pew racks for visitors to register their attendance.

Dear Florence,

God loves you! I love you! You changed my life! You are a little silver box. I have some of your books and tapes. Keep on going.

Love, Carissa

P. S. I enjoy your work.

She also drew a silver box and put an arrow toward it in case I might miss the connection.

The Regazzi family has been listening to my Personality Plus tapes for years, and when I spoke at Andrews University, they were all in the front row. They took me to their home, and I became acquainted with their two children, Marla (16) and Mark (12). Later Marla wrote:

13

Dear Mrs. Littauer,

It seems strange to address you as "Mrs. Littauer" for around our home you are simply "Florence." To me you are like a friend or the next door neighbor. You are an indispensable part of my life. A favorite phrase of our family was: Is that affirming? I'm sure it will now become: Is that edifying? It was a privilege to spend a few personal moments with you. Thank you so very much for all the silver boxes with bows that you graciously gave to me.

Love, Marla

Seventeen-year-old Keri Simms wrote me:

Florence,

I went to a Southern Baptist Convention camp this fall called "Freefall." At this camp we were split up into smaller groups in which we had Bible studies every day. At the end of the weekend, we were asked to each take a piece of paper, put our name on it, and sign each other's paper saying something nice about everyone.

Even though we were assigned to do this, each time I get low I take out that paper and read those comments. Those people I had only known 72 hours gave me silver boxes with bows on top. They are very special to me. It is easy sometimes to say things to people you know. But when people who didn't know me very well said, "You care, you listen, and you have a beautiful loving smile which shows Jesus in your life" that hits me every time I read it. That was a huge silver box with a bow on it just for me.

Keri Simms

Bright children really want to learn about themselves and how to improve their personalities if only someone can present the information in a way that is both simple and entertaining. In my book *Raising the Curtain on Raising Children*, I have shown parents and grandparents how to teach about the personalities and make it fun. I am constantly amazed at how little children who have heard my tapes and been encouraged by their parents will come to an all-day seminar, listen, and take notes.

Little Amanda Thar is only eight years old. She not only had listened to the tapes, but she came to hear the Sunday message on silver boxes. Later she sent me a handmade Valentine and a note. On her drawing, she has the M (Melancholy) tidying up the house. The S (Sanguine) is supposed to be me on a stage speaking next to a table covered with silver boxes with bows on top. The F (Amanda's abbreviation for Phlegmatic) is resting on the sand in the sun. And the K (Choleric) is the teacher by her big desk, telling the children what to do. At her early age, Amanda has a grasp on the personalities that will help her to understand her family and friends, and she knows the value of a little silver box with a bow on top.

When John was eleven years old, he first came to hear me speak on the personalities. At each break in the seminar, John would come up to talk with me, and I would tell him how amazed I was that someone his age was willing to sit all day Saturday and learn how to understand himself and others. John and I became friends, and each time I'm in Arizona, John appears even if it's a women's seminar. He stands by the back table and tells people about the different tapes and books.

For the last two years, his mother has come to the Southern California Women's Retreat and brought John along. Even though he is obviously not a woman, we let him sit in the back when I'm speaking and assist my husband with the books. After this year's retreat, John's mother wrote,

Florence, you have given me and my immediate family so many silver boxes, and our John shares your boxes with all he comes in contact with. He spread the personality information to his grandmother and aunt last summer. Then in Boy Scouts he learned to be a counselor and was trained to be a Junior Leader. In all this he has used your teachings to help others and to help himself understand others, so he can get along better with difficult people.

John recently attended the Meeting of the Men, a men's retreat we sponsored in Irvine, California. He was the youngest attendee and one of the most enthusiastic. I adore young John, who is now fourteen, and I know his willingness to learn and share will give him a tremendous advantage in personal relationships as he matures.

Not only do little children pay attention when I speak about the boxes, but teenagers, a group who often work at being bored by sermons, seem fascinated with the idea that their words could possibly be of value.

They also are very quick to give me examples of people who have either helped or hurt them with their words.

Jeanine wrote me that people made fun of her, saying she was fat:

> I was really hurting badly inside, and it finally got to me so much I stopped eating for two days. I went to my youth pastor, and he told me positive things about myself. He showed me he really cared, and it didn't matter to him what I looked like. He gave me 'Silver Boxes.' He's the only one really that I can go to. He made me find the good things in myself when I was seriously considering suicide. I think his Silver Boxes are so beautiful, and I'm glad he gives them to me.

Then she added a teenager's P.S.

You're a very good speaker. You have helped me. I like your dresses too. I hope this letter is a silver box for you in some way. Please take care.

"And whoso shall receive one such little child in my name receiveth me. But whoso shall offend one of these little ones which believe in me, it were better for him that a millstone were hanged about his neck, and that he were drowned in the depth of the sea" (Matthew 18:5–6).

4

Gift Boxes

On January 1, 1988, I sent out my New Year's letter. Somehow I had missed writing at Christmas, and so I started the year by suggesting that we give out kind words in silver boxes to our family and friends instead of just material gifts.

I don't remember many of the presents I received as a child, but I recall some encouraging words. My father taught me vocabulary and instilled in me a love for the English language. Aunt Sadie said, "You can learn to play the piano." She taught me: I learned, and I played the wedding march at her marriage to Charlie, the upholsterer. Miss Croston, my English teacher, chose me to enter the poetry reading contest: she coached me and I won. Aunt Jean encouraged me to apply for a scholarship to college: she helped me fill out the forms, I was awarded full tuition, and I followed in her footsteps to become an English teacher.

I don't recall who gave me paper dolls, but I remember the encouraging words from loving people who gave me little silver boxes with bows on the top. As I speak each day, I want my words to be more than entertaining and exhorting. I want them to encourage others to become the very best they can be. That's why I train others to be speakers and leaders—"yes, you can do it . . . you have something to say . . . you are a person of value . . . God can use you to encourage others."

As we start the new year of 1988, let's think of which people could use some silver boxes from us, and let's give them verbal gifts with bows on top.

To you, our friends and family, we "hear of your love, and of the faith which you have toward the Lord Jesus" and we are encouraged as you have given us "much joy and comfort in your love because the hearts of the saints have been refreshed through you" (Philemon 5 and 7, NASB).

The response to this message was beyond anything I had experienced in my thirty-five years of sending yearly letters, and it gave me the impetus to continue working on the silver box subject and ultimately turn it into a book.

The first response was from my Aunt Jean, my deceased mother's sister. From the time I was a child, I had admired Aunt Jean. She had graduated from Tufts College with high honors and had become an English teacher. As our family struggled through the depression, living in the three little rooms behind my father's store, Aunt Jean married a man of means and moved into a real house, the type I dreamed of: white Cape Cod style with green shutters, a huge front yard where we could play croquet, and a public park with rose gardens nearby. Uncle Ethan planted strawberries, blueberries, and raspberries; and grew trees producing apples, plums, peaches, and cherries; and could feed the neighborhood on his peas, beans, corn, tomatoes, and zucchini. Going to visit Aunt Jean and Uncle Ethan was the highlight of my childhood summers.

As I grew up, it was Aunt Jean who encouraged me to go to college. We had similar personalities and the same sense of humor, and I wanted to be like her. She was my role model, and I followed in her footsteps. My scholarship to the University of Massachusetts brought me to the western part of the state within easy distance of her home. Even though I didn't have a car, I often found friends who were willing to drive me to Westfield to enjoy one of Aunt Jean's home-cooked meals and a fresh cherry pie.

Aunt Jean helped me select my courses and encouraged me to become an English teacher like her. She was my second mother and later a second grandmother to my children. She inspired us all to achieve and often said, "Of course you can do it!"

Since my mother's death, Aunt Jean has become the senior member of my family. My brothers and I keep in touch with her and see that she gets to the family weddings and funerals. Her response to my Silver Box letter was very touching. She wrote first that "yesterday's mail was a bonanza!" She had received something from each one of us and was very grateful.

I sometimes think I wouldn't know what to do without Katie's branch of the family; and in light of the New Year's message you sent yesterday, you three children (you, Jim, and Ron) are the silver boxes with bows on top that your mother left to me! I love you all and am so proud of the contributions you have been able to make. I've often stressed in my devotions that each of us should strive to make this world a little better place because he or she passed this way, and the Chapman contingent is certainly doing just that.

Tears of gratitude came to my eyes as I saw in writing that Aunt Jean considered me a silver box with a bow on top.

Sometimes we think of compliments as great meaningful sentences of praise and don't realize that the two words *thank you* can give a blessing to others. Our good friend, Jan Frank, author of *Door of Hope*, told me that her husband Don had made a fire for her one evening. She usually took his thoughtfulness for granted but that night gave him a simple thank you. The next day Don hugged her and said, "You gave me a silver box last night when you thanked me for making a fire."

Later Don taught the silver box lesson to his high school class. The class is made up of boys who have been discipline problems in school, and many of them come from dysfunctional families. They liked the idea of receiving praise, and soon they were giving silver boxes to each other. We may never know what benefits these young people received from these unaccustomed words of affirmation from their teacher and from each other, but there may be one of them who in future years looks back and says, "It was that teacher with the silver boxes who changed the direction of my life."

When Bev Lane was eighteen, in college, and looking for direction, a counselor named Adele told her about a camp where sixth graders go for outdoor education. As Bev got excited about helping at this camp, she exclaimed, "Perhaps I could go as a dishwasher." The counselor looked her straight in the eye and said, "Yes, you could be a dishwasher, but I believe you would be a great counselor with those kids." Bev was stunned that Adele had this kind of confidence in her because she was unsure of herself and a little scared of tackling a leadership role. She said to herself, "If Adele believes in me, then maybe this could be true."

That encouragement came twenty-five years ago, and it led Bev to one and a half years of counseling at that camp before going back to college and becoming a teacher. She found that she had a God-given ability to work with children, and she is still doing it. In her own words, "Just last year I went back to that very same educational camp with my sixth-grade class, and this time I came, not as a dishwasher or as a cabin leader, but as a professional teacher. It was a beautiful time—a gift—a silver box with a bow on it. Someone years ago (Adele) believed in me when I didn't believe in myself—and it changed my life."

Few of us realize the difference that a word from us can make in a life. Nancy Peavey is a petite, adorable girl from Baton Rouge. When she was first married, she says, "I was very skinny and insecure. No one had ever really helped me see value in me."

Nancy's mother, sensing her depression, gave Nancy a copy of *I'm Out to Change My World* by Ann Kiemel. Nancy stayed up all night to read it, and she sensed Ann's faith was far different from hers and that she seemed to have joy even in adverse circumstances. When Nancy heard Ann was coming to Baton Rouge to speak at her church, she got excited and went to hear her. Afterwards Nancy drew a charcoal picture and called to ask if she could bring it to Ann. In Nancy's words:

Ann was so touched that she cried. I stayed just a short time, but when I got ready to go Ann walked me to my car

She wrapped her arms around me and said, 'I love you, Nancy.' I couldn't believe it—she loved skinny, insecure me. It was as though Jesus had said it because it felt unconditional. I came home that night in December, fell to my knees and gave myself to Him 100 percent, no middle of the road. He could add or take away anything from my life. I was His.

I wrote Ann and thanked her for what she had shown me and said she never had to write me again. I could be *love* right in Baton Rouge, Louisiana. In other words, I could pass on what she showed me—Christ's love. Well, she wrote me back, and we've written for fourteen years now. I even attended her wedding in Boston. We just keep sending silver boxes through the mail.

Nancy now lives in California and is one of my daughter Marita's best friends. Not knowing anything about her experience with Ann, I have hugged her and encouraged her. She has come to CLASS (Christian Leaders and Speakers Seminar) where I tried to help her see her potential. This past year, she has been teaching Personality Plus at her church. When we first met, she thought she was a melancholy personality, but with closer study and evaluation, she found she had been a depressed Sanguine—a person whose desire was for fun but whose circumstances had held her down. As she has found her true identity, she has become a happy person teaching others how to understand themselves.

I'm sure Ann had no idea that her simple, "I love you, Nancy," would cause Nancy to go to her knees and commit her life to the Lord. Nor did I know when I hugged Nancy and told her she could be a speaker that my attention changed her motivation. Then she wrote me, "As long as I live, I will be amazed at how God brought us together. It was so in his plan for Marita and me to meet and become friends. I really do feel kindred spirits with you and Marita. I feel as though we've always known each other. God has shown love to me in such a great way through you. I am overwhelmed."

So often we think that to be encouragers we have to produce great words of wisdom when, in fact, a few simple syllables of sympathy and an arm around the shoulder can often provide much needed comfort in a sad situation. Ceci Anthis, after hearing me speak on Silver Boxes, later wrote of her son's comforting words and actions.

In the last four years, I have gone through a lot of "rejection" after a job related disability. At the same time, my daughter Rachel was having major medical problems, and our family really entered a "desert period." There were many moments of really needing to feel loved, appreciated, and needed!

On one such day, my son walked up to me, looked in my eyes, and simply said, *"Mom, is it time for a hug?"* I was instantly transformed from lonely despair to feeling loved and cared about. Someone had noticed my need!

This simple but effective little silver box with a bow on top has continued to be *our* special way of acknowledging that we are aware of each others' emotional needs and that we *are there for each other!* Joel is now fourteen, and our relationship draws closer each time we share and open-up to each other.

You see, when we give that silver box to each other, we "open it," and by so doing we really have developed a great understanding of each other's needs and emotional weaknesses. I don't think we would ever have established the honest, open relationship and communication we have now without this special gift to each other.

After Brenda Hollis' husband left her, she felt devastated. Her heart was broken as she thought about her family being separated and never being whole again. She did her best to maintain family functions: birthday parties, holiday celebrations, fun times together. She claimed Galatians 6:9, "Let us not become weary in doing good, for at the proper time we will reap a harvest if we do not give up" (NIV). One by one her daughters later came to her and thanked her for working to make the home a pleasant place in which to be, even while she was grieving. Brenda encourages others by saying, "If we do what's right, God will take care of the future. My daughters have become my silver boxes from God."

Vicki came to the Southern California Women's Retreat and later wrote me about the impact the "Silver Boxes" message had on her life:

> While I sat listening to your talk on that Sunday at the Marriott, the Lord reached out to me through your words to give me a gift—that of understanding, or rather, *experiencing*, for the first time in my life what it really means to encourage others. Through your illustrations I fully grasped the power that my words have on others—either to hurt or to heal.
>
> I began to recognize that every single time I open my mouth I have a choice to make—to encourage, uplift, and give hope, or to undermine, discourage, and judge (no matter how slightly).
>
> As you can imagine, during the last few months I've had a multitude of opportunities to exercise that choice daily, both personally (with my husband, daughter, and friends) and professionally.
>
> A week doesn't go by that I don't think about those 'little silver boxes with the bows on top' just as I am about to make an offhand comment or thoughtless remark.
>
> Your talk also inspired me to thank others who have been especially encouraging to me. I ran right out and bought a bunch of little silver boxes with bows on top, and every now and then, I send one as a thank you gift for someone's special words of encouragement. I figured the Lord would want His encouragers to be encouraged to keep encouraging others—and what better way than to thank them for encouraging me! Whew, that was a mouthful!

Anyway, I thank my Lord for using you in such a needed and powerful way, and my prayers continue to be with you and for the lives that will be changed because of your encouraging words!"

As we think about giving out kind words—silver boxes—in place of expensive presents, we would agree with Ralph Waldo Emerson who said, "Rings and jewels are not gifts, but apologies for gifts. The only gift is a portion of thyself." Somehow, in our materialistic society, we have come to equate giving with money and possessions that can be held in our hands. But when we reflect on the turning points in our lives, we often find they came at the encouragement of a person who believed in us, a person who took the time and perhaps the risk to give a portion of himself to someone in need.

One of my husband's favorite books is a little one published in 1947, *Try Giving Yourself Away*[1] by David Dunn. The author had established a hobby so exciting and rewarding that he had to write a book about it, about the art of giving himself away each day in order to encourage or uplift another person, who was often a total stranger. Dunn found great pleasure and fulfillment in looking for ways to give of himself to others. To do this we have to be alert to circumstances and people around us and move quickly to assist them by word or deed. Dunn says, "Opportunities for reaping dividends of happiness are fleeting. You have to act quickly or they elude you. But that only adds zest."[2] Dunn's 110 pages are full of his personal examples of giving himself away and the amazing responses he received when he made himself into a Silver Box with a bow on top. He turned his selfless giving into a hobby which I would like to recommend for each one of us.

Every day Fred and I look for ways to brighten up the life of the weary desk clerk, the stressed-out stewardess, the plodding waitress, the burned-out pastor, the abandoned wife, the lonely lady in line. It's much easier to avoid them all and look the other way, but what a joy it is when you strike that spark in a dark life and see a smile spread across the face.

Giving yourself away is the opposite of looking to see what can be grabbed out of life, but it is far more rewarding and may even be used by God to change another person's life.

As you continue reading this book, we will show you the results of giving both encouraging and discouraging words and challenge you to be a giver of silver boxes. Why not make it a hobby as David Dunn suggested:

> It is a fascinating hobby. Like collecting anything else, you are always looking for new experiences in giving-away to add to your collection. Unlike other forms of collecting, however, you need no safe or cabinet in which to keep your treasures; nor do you have to go out of your way to keep adding to your collection. You have only to look around, wherever you are, to discover some opportunity to give yourself away.
>
> I recommend giving-away as an exciting and thoroughly satisfying hobby. In fact, if you will give it a good try, I'll practically guarantee you a happier life—starting right away![3]

"A word spoken in due season, how good it is!" (Proverbs 15:23, NKJV).

5

Secret Boxes

*H*umanly speaking, my kind of personality likes to get credit for doing good works. I've always been the caretaker of people who needed help and have never hesitated to jump in quickly and administer emotional first aid. I always assumed it was natural to desire accolades for such sacrificial dedication, and I usually got them. When I first started studying the Bible seriously and began to apply the principles to my everyday life, I was stopped in my little spiritual tracks by a verse in the Good News Bible. "When you help a needy person, do it in such a way that even your closest friend will not know about it" (Matthew 6:3, TEV).

That command seemed like an impossibility to me at the time. I was a great giver of silver boxes, but I wanted you to open my shiny presents in front of a party full of people and give praises unto my name.

The next verse went on to say: "Then it will be a private matter. And your Father, who sees what you do in private, will reward you" (Matthew 6:4, TEV).

This spiritual principle was so foreign to my nature at the time that I had to pray about even the possibility I could give secretly. To make my philanthropies private matters and go on the chance that God would mysteriously reward me at some future time was completely out of character for me. God convicted me of this desire for my life, so I did what I always do: I began to teach it to others letting them know that I was in the process of making this real in my own life.

I started with teaching my children the value of giving without looking for credit and showed them that what we did in secret God would reward openly. To break a lifelong habit is not easy, and there were many times when I would hear myself saying to my children, "See what Mother has done today? . . . Did you notice I picked up all your things you left strewn around the house? . . . Wasn't I good to let your friend stay overnight? . . . Look at all the laundry I did for you."

I had not realized before I began to break the habit, what a habit it really was. If I do and you praise, I will continue to do. After a period of visible effort on my part, the children joined in, and when I would ask for affirmation, they would give it to me, "Noble Mother to do these great works." I would smile proudly, and then they would add, "It's a shame you got the credit here, for now you won't receive it in heaven." As we joined together in good humor, we all learned in a practical way that we are commissioned to give without looking for credit. We are to lavish silver boxes on everyone and not stay around to watch them unwrap the blessings.

One night I spoke on Matthew 6:3, 4 at the California Women's Retreat at the Concord Hilton. Later, a bellman came to my room with a gift. On a tray was a lavish display of flowers, a plate of cheese and crackers, a women's magazine, and a Valentine. Written on the card was this note:

> Although we've never met, you've changed my life through your wonderful taped messages. I can hardly wait to meet you in person. Heeding your advice that a "true giver" doesn't even tell her best friend, I haven't, but I wonder how does it really feel not knowing who your secret admirer is? Can you stand it?

I could hardly stand it. The next day I thanked the mystery giver from the platform and applauded her personal application of Matthew 6:3, 4. I explained that even though I was praising her publicly, she would still get her credit in heaven because I wasn't announcing her name—after all, I didn't know it.

Since I began speaking on silver boxes, many people have shared quietly with me about those who have helped them at a time of need and have not looked for credit.

Doris Gibbos told me of a tragic time in her life. In December of 1962, she had four little children and was seven months pregnant with the fifth, when her husband was killed in an automobile accident. Friends and relatives came to support her through the initial shock, but soon after the funeral people went back to their routines and Doris was left to get over her grief as best she could. There was a brief burst of interest when the new baby arrived, but in general no one mentioned her loss.

Doris remembers well the one person who consistently cared—her late husband's former office receptionist. Here was a lady who had no obligation to encourage the grieving widow, but who called every day for over three months. She didn't talk long; she just checked on how Doris was doing and let her know she was thinking of her. Doris said of this quiet giver, "She was such a blessing and encouragement to me when I felt like my life was over."

Having lost two sons of my own, I know how abandoned an individual feels during a time of grieving. It isn't that our friends don't love us anymore; it's that they are uncomfortable around us because they don't know what to say. Our daughter Lauren, who lived through this period of grief with us, and who later suffered the loss of one of her own babies, has written a sensitive book that will help everyone who reads it: *What You Can Say When You Don't Know What to Say*.

By learning how to handle difficult situations, we can be better used of the Lord to be compassionate comforters to others.

In today's busy world full of hurting people, there are so few who are either able or willing to listen to someone's problems and uphold them in time of need. In our new book, *Freeing Your Mind from Memories That Bind*, Fred and I suggest as part of the restoration process from the adult pains of childhood abuse that each person give away at least one silver box a day and be willing to put an arm around some other individual and say, "I care."

Isaiah 40:1, 2 tells us "'Comfort, comfort my people,' says your God. 'Speak tenderly to Jerusalem'" (RSV).

Comforting and speaking tenderly are not easy things to do, and they get little visible credit from the Christian community, but there is a desperate need today for people who care to give a silver box here or there without expecting any credit in return. Even when you are hurting yourself, giving out an encouraging word to someone else can lift your spirits.

Wanda Smith had a beautiful experience with a ninety-two-year-old secret giver who was her mother's roommate in the nursing home. Wanda's mother Sara was, at fifty-two, a victim of Alzheimer's disease, and Wanda had a five-year struggle of caring for her. She prayed daily for help, comfort, and companionship, but no one seemed to care.

One day Wanda walked into the room where her mother had been for a year, and the frail ninety-two-year-old roommate was gone. "I thought she'd died," Wanda wrote. "I'd always liked her because whenever I came in, she'd wake up and talk. Whether it was at midnight, at breakfast, or in the middle of the afternoon, she'd smile and ask me how I was doing."

That day Wanda took her mother for a ride down the hall and noticed the little old lady sitting in a corner, weeping. Wanda stopped and asked her what was wrong. She cried,

"They've taken me out of your mother's room. If I can't be in with Sara, I might as well die." Wanda couldn't imagine why she would care, since Sara couldn't walk, talk, move, or respond to anyone. Why would this woman want to be with an unresponsive person when she could be in a room with someone who could converse?

"Why do you need to live near Sara?" Wanda asked.

The reply from this caring lady was a silver box in itself. "God needs me to make sure the nurses take care of Sara."

Here was a sainted lady who took it as her responsibility to care for Sara, to call the nurses when they were needed, to be a guardian angel to someone who couldn't possibly thank her.

Wanda said about this lady, "She saved up silver boxes for 365 days that year and gave them to me all at once. God answered my prayer."

And I'm sure God will reward the little lady with her own silver boxes in heaven.

One woman wrote that she had started a silver box ministry to the teens in her church. She had realized that there were many young people who were hurting, who wouldn't talk to any adult authority figure, and yet who needed mature counsel.

She says:

> I have a small ministry now of silver boxes as I work with our High School pastor to write to the various kids in the youth department who are hurting, who are friendless, who don't realize that God loves them. . . . I am the Secret Angel! My identity is truly a secret, and I have written hundreds of letters to various teens who are falling apart. I have received many answers from them (letters addressed to the Secret Angel and left with the youth pastor) and feel that God has truly blessed this work. I tell them they are loved, give them some Scripture related to what is troubling them, and then pray for

them and remind them that God has wonderful plans for their lives and will always be with them. I close with assurances that they are special and that I love them. This is a major joy to me—to give out silver boxes with bows on top!

What a blessing these young people are experiencing because one Secret Angel is willing to spend time creatively ministering to those in need without any chance of praise or credit.

Many people go to seminars and spend some time in the unfamiliar intimacy of a small group of new friends whom they will probably never see again. In the closing moments some exchange addresses and pledge to keep in touch, but few do. Jeffie was different. As a seventy-year-old widow who had been a pastor's wife and lifelong Bible teacher, Jeffie didn't need to come to CLASS at all. She knew how to communicate effectively, and some people with her credentials might have been a little smug or possibly let the others in their small group know they were just there for the fellowship.

But Jeffie was really different. She said nothing about her years as a spiritual giant, she quietly affirmed the staff leader's comments, and she mothered all those who were terrified of even standing up and reciting their names.

During the three days of CLASS, she became acquainted with each member of her small group and got their addresses. As different ones stood up to share their mini-messages with the others in the group, she took notes about their life stories, personal interests, and positive physical features. The amazing thing about Jeffie was that she did her busy work in such a quiet way that no one noticed her note taking. She hugged, complimented, and challenged her new friends without drawing attention to her own talents. At the end of the three small-group sessions, Jeffie was the most loved person there.

A few weeks after she had returned to Texas from our CLASS in California, she wrote each person a letter telling what she had noticed about them at their first meeting, what line they had delivered that was most memorable, and what she loved about their looks and personality. If they had expressed any problem or concern, she asked about it and assured them she was praying for their needs.

Although her writing may not sound unusual, the response was. The group members who wrote back said they couldn't believe Jeffie remembered their life stories or cared enough to write to someone when she didn't have to.

Several commented that they would never have thought of doing what Jeffie did. Most touching, however, were the letters from those who wrote that they had never before received a note of encouragement, written out of love and concern, not obligation—or any correspondence, for that matter, that was affirming and didn't ask them for anything.

What a sad commentary on our lifestyle today that a silver box given with no expectation of anything in return is so unusual as to cause the recipient shock and disbelief.

Sometimes just saying hello to someone can be a silver box, even if we don't give a recognizable compliment. So many people are so lonely that any token of attention would be encouraging. One night our CLASS staff went out for dinner, and as we all settled in at a long table, I noticed a lady sitting all by herself in a nearby booth. I felt led to speak to her, so I went over and introduced myself. She asked me to sit down, so I did. She told me she was a business teacher at the local high school. I explained that CLASS was a seminar for Christian leaders and speakers, and she was quite interested to hear what we did. I asked her how often she ate at this restaurant, and she said, "Almost every night."

I couldn't imagine eating alone in the same booth in the same restaurant every night for years. When I got up to leave, she thanked me for coming over and concluded, "I'm alone here every night and you're the first person who has ever come to the booth and spoken to me who wasn't a waitress."

Giving away a silver box is often as easy as a simple nod or a hello. My husband Fred could win an award on how many times a day he says hello to strangers in elevators, opens doors for ladies with bundles, picks up what someone has dropped, and cheers up downcast waitresses. He whistles joyfully in banks and stores and is frequently asked, "Why are you so happy today?" The fact that this question is even asked shows how few people are giving out positive thoughts or even smiles to others. Fred has what we call a Cosmetics Counter Ministry. He loves different colognes and has a collection of miniatures that are given away at cosmetics counters. His ministry started as he would be sampling fragrances and the salesperson would ask him why he was so happy. She would praise him and compare him to all the other grouchy people she had to deal with in a given day.

Within minutes he would be sharing his faith in the Lord, listening to her own personal tale of woe, showing compassion for her circumstances, giving her answers, and often praying with her right there over the counter. Fred has found that he is able to pursue his hobby and give out silver boxes at the same time. Often when I return to the cosmetics counter, I find Fred just where I left him. If he says, "This is your new sister," I know he has led her to the Lord. Or sometimes he tells me later that she has been a Christian for ten years but needed some affirmation of her faith. Always, he gives me a comment that indicates what he has been able to do in the heart of one clerk in thirty minutes. Often he goes to the car and gets one of my books to start her off in the right direction. As she gives him samples of sweet smelling fragrances, he gives her silver boxes, encouraging words that may change the course of her life.

"You can be sure that whoever gives even a drink of cold water to one of the least of these my followers because he is my follower, will certainly receive a reward" (Matthew 10:42, TEV).

The opposite of giving out secret silver boxes is giving compliments only when you are sure of receiving credit or when the receiver is worthy in stature or deserving of praise.

Frequently Fred and I arrive at hotels or churches and mingle with the group of guests before they know who we are. It is amazing how frequently people will glance at us, register a look of "Who are you?" and then turn away without even a hello.

One night we arrived at a large Christian convention in a lovely hotel. We were standing in the hall when the doors opened and a workshop group was let out. Fred and I smiled and nodded to the people as they strolled by, but no one spoke to us. When they had all left, we read the title on the door and found that these people had just been trained in "The Techniques of Personal Evangelism." I don't know whether evangelism was narrowed down to the jungles of Africa or to a one-week church outreach program in a restricted community, but obviously they were not taught to smile at strangers in hotel lobbies.

Frequently before I speak, a man appears from some back room holding a lavalier mike and the battery pack that goes with it. Sometimes if I don't have a belt or a pocket, I have to attach the clip of the battery pack to the top of my pantyhose, necessitating my backing into a secluded corner or retreating to the ladies' room. As I explain all this to the audio man, we have a chance to get acquainted. After the program, I try to seek out the man and thank him for his help and courtesy. The sadly amazing response is often, "You are the first speaker who's ever thanked me. All I ever get is complaints. I get the blame when the mikes don't work, but I never get any credit when they're right."

One professional audio man told me, "The more important or well-known the singer or speaker is, the worse they treat us. In their eyes we are nonpersons."

Isn't it odd that some of us can present the gospel in song or word, but offstage look down on those that don't appear worthy of our time. How little it takes to give a silver box to a quiet servant of the Lord.

Another thing we have learned is that people at conventions speak only to those who are wearing nametags identifying them as part of the group. Somehow they don't want to waste their words on people who don't belong. No nametag, no fellowship.

One morning Fred and I sat at a large round table at the breakfast meeting of a Christian convention. We both greeted the group and smiled pleasantly. We gave our names, but everyone was so caught up in what a woman on the opposite side of the table was saying that no one ever spoke to us. And when Fred got up and poured coffee, he was thanked mechanically as if he were the waiter. When it was time for me to speak, I went to the platform. When I was through, one lady at our table exclaimed, "Why didn't you tell us you were somebody!" She then turned to the others and said, "Imagine, we had the speaker right here at our table, and we never knew it."

I was grateful that I was the speaker, for if I had been an agnostic news reporter, I might not have had much good to say about the warm and gracious spirit of Christian hospitality.

One night as I arrived to speak at a banquet and walked by the registration table, a lady stopped me and tried to hand me a nametag. I smiled and said, "I don't need a nametag." Staunch in her sense of duty, she said sternly, "I didn't ask you if you wanted a nametag; I told you to put it on."

I was a little surprised at her tone, and as I looked down at this large orange pumpkin that she was trying to thrust upon me, I said, "It doesn't really go with my pink dress." She put her hands on her hips and stated clearly, "We did not design these nametags to coordinate with your outfit."

I could see I was engaged in a losing battle, so I took the pumpkin and wended my way to the head table. The lady went on with her dedicated task of pinning pumpkins on the guests and didn't look my way again until the chairman called the meeting to order and introduced the head table. When I was named as the speaker, I watched the reaction of the nametag lady. Her mouth dropped open, and she almost lost control of her handful of pumpkins.

Once the meal was underway, this lady stooped down and tried to make her way inconspicuously along the back of the head table until she got to me. She assured me that I didn't really have to wear the pumpkin on my pink dress if I didn't want to. "If I'd only known you were the speaker, I wouldn't have spoken to you that way." I assured her I wasn't upset. Once again I felt grateful that this had happened to me, the speaker, instead of a first-timer who had walked in alone, looking for love.

Actually, I found just such a person in the ladies' room when I went to freshen up before speaking. She had come into the hotel to go to the singles' bar. She was a lonely, young widow who was desperate for some relief from her grief. I invited her in to listen to my testimony, and she was willing to come. I marched her right by the registration table and the nametag lady, who smiled weakly and did not try to thrust a pumpkin on this tagless lady.

The lady wept through the part of my story where I told of how my two sons died, and she prayed with me at the end to ask the Lord Jesus into her life to change her and to fill the emptiness in her heart. Afterward she thanked me for rescuing her from the singles' bar and for changing her direction for the evening and for life. I introduced her to a committee member who happened to live in her area, and they became instant friends.

That night we proved it is possible to lead to the Lord someone who has not paid to get in, who is not a part of the group, and who isn't even wearing a nametag.

As I walked into an evening meeting and banquet, I greeted everyone in the receiving line that was stretched out along the wall. When I got to the end of the line I noticed a quiet lady who was obviously there by herself. I exchanged a few words with her before being led to the head table by the chairman. The people were instructed to take a seat, and I noticed the lonely lady sat right in front of me. Each time I looked down from the platform where the head table had been placed, I noticed that no one at her table was talking with her. In fact, they had actually turned their backs on her and were conversing around her. I asked the chairman if she knew this lady, and she responded that she was not part of their church group.

When it was dessert time, I excused myself from the head table and went down to where this lady was sitting. The chair across from her was empty, and I sat down. I found out she was the daughter of a pastor of a different denomination and had planned to come with her mother who at the last minute was detained. As I talked with her, the other ladies noticed I was there and turned toward me all excited that I had come to their table. I introduced them to this lady and suggested they get to know her. They explained that they were all from one church and wanted to have fun together, but they did at least include her for the few minutes left before I spoke. Later the lady thanked me for noticing she was alone and speaking to her.

So few people, even fine Bible-quoting Christians, make it a point to reach out to someone they don't know. If the person doesn't have on a nametag, is an obvious outsider, doesn't seem to fit into their group, or—heaven forbid—looks a little peculiar or eccentric, we tend to turn the other way and let them fall where they may.

Sometimes giving out a silver box is as simple as acknowledging a person's presence and saying hello.

"In her tongue is the law of kindness" (Proverbs 31:26).

6

Mailboxes

Some of the most encouraging words I've received have been written ones, notes from friends who care, cards of joy and cheer. There's something special about the written word that can be read over and over again. Anna Garrity keeps my speaking schedule at her desk, and she times her notes to coincide with my return home. When I walk in late at night, tired from a long trip, I can count on an encouraging note from Anna. It's not a long letter about her problems, although she is not free of them; it's not a chronicle of her children's achievements; it's a few lines of understanding and a renewed commitment to pray for me. As I am writing this week, hidden away by myself, I received these words from Anna:

> I shall pray for you every day this week as you write. I love all your books, and I know that much has to go into them for so much of God's love, healing, and wisdom to come out of them. May God bless and guide your writing this week and may all your dreams come true.

I have Anna's note in front of me as I write. It is a silver box with a bow on top.

Anita Sepp wrote me of how she values her husband's thoughtful notes and gifts.

> I am mother of two preschoolers and a wife of a busy USAF officer. It goes without saying, I often have long, exhausting days. My husband periodically stops by the flower shop on the way home from work and buys flowers for me (nothing fancy, just a daisy or two). With the flowers always

comes a most precious thing—a card. These cards are not elaborate or expensive (in fact, they're the free ones given out by the florist). I treasure these cards which range from "I appreciate you" to "You're doing a great job with the kids" to "You're a precious wife." Sometimes they're funny cards. One day he gave me a get-well card. I was shocked because I was feeling especially great that day. But I read on, "Get well . . . prepared for a great life together." I keep all these cards in a box in my kitchen, and whenever I am down or discouraged, I go to this box to receive hope and joy which is worth more than any *thing!*

What a blessing to have a good man who gives out silver boxes. What an encouragement to have the cards handy to reread whenever Anita needs a pick-up on a down day.

Few of us stop to realize the value of the written word. It takes so little actual time to put a few encouraging comments on a piece of paper.

Gilda Gearhart wrote a special Valentine message to her husband this year instead of just signing her name to a ready-made card. He was touched by her loving and creative words, and as he read it, he smiled and said, "This is so good you should write a book."

Leslie Pilkington wrote about a friend who encouraged her when she was lonely and resistant to the efforts of others to encourage her.

"I had a friend Marlene who kept sending me cards and balloons and kept calling me. She was the first true friend I had had since I was five. I was pretty hard to approach, but Marlene kept trying and reaching out to me. Finally I was able to respond to her and be her friend and give to her. Because of her, I am now free to reach out to others. I am no longer afraid. She encouraged me with Scripture to press on in the Lord—and I am!"

Sometimes when we reach out to someone and they don't respond, we feel we've done our Christian duty, so we check them off our mental list, and we move on to more exciting projects. If we stop and think about it, we will realize that the most hurting people are the least apt to be responsive to our encouraging words. Often, extremely depressed people won't answer the phone or open the front door, but they will usually read their mail.

Emilie Barnes, who is as busy in her traveling ministry as I am, never ceases to amaze me at the number of handwritten notes she sends out each week. She keeps notepaper with her at all times, and she can dash off several notes while waiting for a plane. She has little cards that she uses and sells at her book table that say, "I love you because _____." The person writing has only to add a sentence or two of personalized thoughts and mail it off. Emilie writes them to her husband Bob and leaves them for him to find in his sock drawer, work bench, or Bible. The response she receives from the use of these cards is amazing as people write and tell her how thrilled their mate, mother, child, or friend was to have proof of their love and how they carry the card around with them to read over and over again.

Mary Jo remembers a silver box she got from Emilie Barnes. Emilie was her group leader at CLASS, and Emilie is a master giver of silver boxes. She has a prayer basket that she keeps with her during her prayer time every day. In that basket are little cards on which she can write a brief note to those she has prayed for. One day Mary Jo got one of these notes which said simply, "Mary Jo, I prayed for you today."

Mary Jo went on to tell me that she still has this little "silver box" from Emilie. She said, "I think Emilie does not know how to live without giving silver boxes in all shapes and forms. When she exhales, silver bows come out. She is truly an inspiration."

Emilie has one unique way of sending silver boxes that I have never seen done anywhere else. Its unexpectedness makes it all the more special. If you go to her home for dinner, you will be treated to an evening to remember. You may have split pea soup with ham hocks, or you may have her famous overnight turkey recipe, but you can be sure that you will have great food and fellowship. While you are still fasting to lose the extra pounds you picked up at her party, Emilie has taken a few minutes after doing the dishes to drop you a simple note thanking you for coming to her home to eat her food! I have been continually amazed that while I am still thinking *I need to write her a thank-you note,* I get one in the mail from her!

Dana Berry wrote this tribute to her mother:

On my graduation night from high school, my mother gave me a letter, the first one I ever got from her. It was a beautiful letter. (I had no idea she could write so beautifully.) It was just to thank me for not giving her any worry while I grew up and for bringing laughter into our home. Then she went on to tell me she would always support me in my life ahead and that she felt that even if I didn't do anything big and wonderful in life that just being me would be enough. I still have the letter, and that is my silver box. She really loves me!

How much we all long for written proof that "somebody really loves me."

Any time a man is going through difficult financial troubles, he is in special need of uplifting words from his mate. So often we women retreat at such a time and feel we are being noble because we haven't "spoken our mind." Adversity either brings us closer together in mutual need and support or tears apart an already shaky marriage. The majority of the couples we counsel in bad times are in the latter category, but I rejoiced when Janet Pohlhammer showed me the following letter of thanks her husband Chuck had written her on Valentine's Day, 1989. It was penned on yellow lined paper with no frills. When I asked if I could use this as a silver box example, Jan said I could as long as I returned it so she could carry it with her forever.

Dear Janet,

No card at the Hallmark store could ever express the feelings I have for you. The past months have been very hard on me. This is the first time in my life that my work world has fallen in on me. There have been bad times when I wanted to quit and did, but never a time when the employer chose not to need me.

Without your support through the lean times, I never could have made it. It seems that adversity has brought us closer and closer.

Thank you for your undying love and perpetual optimism. I really need it. I am going to give this new situation my best, and with your help, I can turn things around. But regardless, I still have you, and that's all that really matters to me.

I love you more every day.

Chuck

It is never too late to send that note of thanks or appreciation. Lois waited for over forty years to hear that her mother thought she was good, to know that her mother was proud of her. She says, "Now, in my mid forties with three children, I continue to feel the need to be approved of." Finally after a successful and elaborate fiftieth anniversary party that Lois put on for her parents, the silver box came.

Lois told me, "A month later I received the most incredible letter from my mother telling me I had given such a big piece of my life to planning their celebration and how lovely and meaningful it was to them. She also mentioned how my love for my Savior was seen in the sweetness of my three boys and had been passed on to them. I read it every week."

It is never too late to send or receive a silver box.

A written word of encouragement can brighten a day and add value to a life. Give them freely, for you never know what a difference you'll make. I doubt that the successful Harvard graduate had any idea how valuable the note he wrote to his friend's wife would be.

Pam shared with me how worthless she had felt after her second child was born:

> I had left my full-time management position to be at home with my children. I felt a loss of self-esteem that having a career gave me, and I succumbed to the values of the Superwoman syndrome. In short, I did not value my place in the home. One day I received an unexpected note from a friend of my husband's encouraging me in my role as a full-time mom. He is a genius and a successful venture capitalist who I never thought put much value on traditional things. He likened me to Christa McAuliffe, the Challenger crew member who taught school. She said "I teach; therefore, I touch the future." I needed to hear that.

A pastor who had not received many silver boxes told me that he had helped a girl in his church get into college. Later she wrote him a thank-you note full of compliments. He has carried it with him ever since, and he said, "When I feel low, I pull out the letter and read it."

The beauty of the written word is that it can be held close to the heart and read over and over again. A spoken silver box may tarnish with the passage of time and the trials of life, but one that is written can be taken out and read and reread. With each reading the glow is enhanced like the finish on fine sterling that gets more beautiful with each polishing. Sherry has a silver box in her Bible that she polishes regularly. She told me, "My friend who discipled me as a new Christian in a new town gave me a Christmas card of encouragement last year that I still carry in my Bible. In her card, she told me that the Lord loves me, that he has a plan for my life, and that the best is yet to come. I love her for giving me a silver box of encouragement—something I had never received from anyone before. Through all my questions and confusion, pain and fear, she always encouraged me."

Some of you may be thinking, *I don't have Emilie's little cards*, or *I don't know how to pray like Anna*, or *I don't have any ability to write*.

What can you do if you want to encourage others but don't have a natural gift of words? You don't know what to say? You don't have many creative ideas?

We all do have something way inside that we'd like to say. We all are born with some amount of creativity. But often we don't know how to put our feelings into words, nor do we think we know what other people would like. Original words giving personal encouragement are the most desirable, but choosing an appropriate card can be an exciting activity and one that will give silver boxes to others.

Sending a card or a note of encouragement can have added bonuses, as this story from Linda points out:

> I used to have a very difficult time picking out a Mother's Day card for my Mother-in-law! She had never really been nice to me and always picked at the things I did. I agonized over which verse to pick on which card. There was nothing to fit her. One time the Lord spoke to me—"Pick the verse the

way you want her to be; I'll do the rest!" So I started choosing cards for her that were beautiful descriptions of the perfect mother-in-law. Over time, she began to become that person. God has begun to change her heart. She really loves me now and even tells others that she loves me. It took God's changing my heart first and my loving her through him!

This was a silver box with a double gift. The receiver feels loved and in return the giver gets an improved relationship. Don't we all know someone we need to send a silver box to?

As I travel and spend time in airports, I go to the gift shops and look over the various regional items and the different brands of greeting cards. In fifteen minutes, I often find the perfect card for a friend or family member. When I go into a supermarket, I stop at the card rack and look over what they have to offer.

In CLASS we teach people who wish to communicate creatively to become "alert to life." By this we mean noticing what's around you that could possibly provide a colorful example. Whether or not you wish to become a speaker, you can increase your Silver Box ministry by being alert to the interests of others. People are delighted when you send them a card or note that refers to something personal in their individual lives, or something that adds to a collection or hobby, or something that just looks like them. To do this effectively, you need to listen to what people say and pick up where their interests lie or what they find amusing.

Over ten years ago, Connie Teilborg put on a Personality Plus seminar in Phoenix. She used frogs for decorations, and her theme was based on the song, "Have you kissed any frogs today? Have you helped anyone along life's way?" The lesson was that if you gave encouraging words to others, you might be used to transform a few frogs into princes. From that time on, Connie and I have been sending each other frogs in any form or shape. The uglier the frog, the more we are amused. When I come home from a long trip and find a box or envelope from Connie, I begin to laugh before I even open it. She has sent me a frog sundial, frog wind chimes, and a frog garden flag. She found a T-shirt with a huge frog on it and a lime green skirt covered with fuschia frogs. Connie can brighten up my day without saying a word.

Recently I received a big box that contained a children's inflatable pool float that was an adorable green frog. My little grandchild Bryan thinks sailing around in Grammie's frog is such fun.

Every time I pass a card rack I see frogs, and I love to find them for unexpected occasions. I've found frogs jumping out of Thanksgiving pumpkins, under Christmas trees, and kissing the Irish Blarney stone. It's amazing when you are alert to life what you can find to cheer on a friend.

Emilie Barnes has a red house converted from a barn and full of nostalgic furnishings. Whenever I see a card with a barn on it, I think of Emilie. Evelyn Davison's ministry theme is "Eve's Apples," so when I see apple cards I get them for her. Missy Chavez loves the concept that Jesus is the shepherd and we are the sheep, so I buy her cards with little wooly lambs. Marilyn Heavilin's first book was *Roses in December,* so whenever I see a card, notepaper, poster, or picture with roses, I get it for her. Recently, she gave me a sterling silver pillbox with roses on it as a reminder of how our ministries have blended together.

This past Christmas a friend gave me a big silver box full of different kinds of silver boxes she had been collecting for me. Some of these little gifts are in the picture on the back cover of this book.

Any card or gift that suits a person's interests will be received with special joy. When I visit in someone's home, I try to observe what they seem to like. A lady in Baltimore had a lighted cabinet with beautiful seashells, so I found a thank you card covered with shells.

I have a friend whose hobby is making miniatures—little houses, stores, churches with tiny furnishings. I happened to see a Christmas card with miniatures, so I got it for her.

Barbara Cooper told me she collected sand, just plain earth, from places she visited. I'd never heard of such a collection, but when I was on the Gold Coast in Australia I thought of her and brought back a sandwich bag full of sand.

From these examples, you get the general idea of how you can branch out into other creative ways to brighten up the life of a friend with an appropriate card or gift.

To remember birthdays and anniversaries, I write dates on a calendar that I keep in my handbag. At the end of each month when I have a few minutes between planes, I look at my list for the next month and try to buy all the cards for each occasion. Sometimes I find ones for the future which I purchase and put in a special file I have for each month. This "tickler file" has a pocket for each month, and I have added sections for thank you cards, baby cards, get-well cards, and sympathy cards. By keeping some in each section, I know that without leaving my office I can reach in and come up with an appropriate card immediately.

As it becomes a way of life to be alert to the interest of others, you will find you have a silver box ministry that will encourage your friends.

Teach your family to commemorate special occasions and to think of unique ways to make other people feel good. As our children were growing up, I encouraged them to decorate for every holiday that came along. Now, it excites me to visit our daughter Lauren's home and see how she involves her three boys in seasonal planning. Traditions are a positive part of raising children and providing them with specific memories that will influence their own home activities in the years to come.

Help your children to have special interests or hobbies that other family members can add to as they grow up and move away. We called Marita "Bunny" when she was little. We let her have a pair of Dutch rabbits as she was growing up, and in her home today, she has a live bunny in a cage. Every time I see a bunny card, figurine, or T-shirt, I get it for Marita.

Lauren has been a little mother all her life. She cared for Marita from the time she was born, and she ministered to our two little brain-damaged boys for months as they had constant seizures and screamed round the clock. She grieved when they no longer could be with us. She has been an exemplary mother to her own three boys and has unfortunately gone through additional grieving over the loss of a much wanted baby girl. Because of her special and deep love for little ones, she collects anything that depicts a loving mother and child: pictures, postcards, and figurines.

Our adopted son Fred has an English bull terrier like TV's Spuds McKenzie, a large white dog with a black spot surrounding one eye. It has always been hard to buy fun things for Fred, but a current crop of bull terrier posters, cards, figurines, T-shirts, and stuffed animals has provided a new and appropriate set of possibilities.

Recently Marita noticed that her brother was lonely from time to time and needed someone to talk to. She decided to let him know that he had a friend, someone he could call at any time of the day or night. Marita watches for appropriate cards to send Fred and every few weeks drops a cute card of encouragement in the mail for him. Sometimes the cards are serious and sometimes they are silly, but Marita has made sure that at least a couple of times a month Fred knows someone cares for him. He's not the type to verbally acknowledge things, but on a recent visit to his office, Marita noticed several of the cards proudly displayed on his desk—silver boxes of encouragement kept out to bring some brightness to his day.

Whether you have a Silver Box ministry of writing notes to those in need, of sending cards to friends, or of giving little appropriate gifts with or without a special occasion, you will be blessed by the lift you give to others.

What fun it was for me to receive a frosty apple for the teacher from Jeffie, a silver box from the ladies at Zion Fellowship, a pair of white socks with red hearts on them for

Valentine's Day from Dana, and a white Irish linen handkerchief with embroidered shamrocks on St. Patrick's Day from Carole.

A gift, word, or card doesn't need to be expensive; it just needs to be encouraging and appropriate and say, "I love you because . . ."

Thank you Fred and Florence
For your invaluable gift
of loving concern
Attractively wrapped in the
silver of personal application
Adorned with colorful ribbons
of self-sacrifice.
My life is enriched through you
and I shall share it.

Marvel Bergland

"My tongue is the pen of a ready writer" (Psalm 45:1).

7

Flower Boxes

When my melancholy son Fred was a child, we were zipping down the freeway toward his school. I looked out the window and noticed the roadway banks all covered with flowers. "Look at all the flowers," I exclaimed. Just at that point, we passed a tall sturdy weed growing amidst the freeway daisies.

"But look at that weed," he said. I was momentarily stopped by what I perceived to be a negative comment. Then, as if he were reading my mind, Fred asked, "Why is it, Mom, that you always see flowers and I seem to see the weeds?"

Why is it that some of us see flowers and others see weeds? Our personalities, our self-worth, our backgrounds, and our circumstances all add together to set our minds on a positive or negative course. When we realize how a weed here or there can choke out our flowers, we will also realize how important it is for us to cultivate the growth of encouraging words. We should be "the sowers of good seed," knowing we will ultimately reap what we sow. Are your planter boxes full of flowers or of weeds?

After attending the Southern California Women's Retreat and hearing me speak on Silver Boxes, including the example of Aunt Jean, Cindy Parsons wrote me a ten-page letter praising her role model, her Aunt Cheri, "who has always been there when I needed her, has always taken an interest in my life, and has always lifted me up with encouraging words: 'You can do it. Look, I did it; so can you. I know it hurts, but time will ease the pain.'"

Cindy recalls her most difficult time in life as the period when her parents were going through a divorce. "My Aunt Cheri rescued me from the pain by her continued efforts to talk with me into the night and even into the early morning. She was there to hold my hand through it, to let me know that she understood the pain and fears and that I could get through it. That was eighteen years ago and the pain is still there, but so is my Aunt Cheri, still showering me with encouraging words."

This same Aunt Cheri gave Cindy realistic advice before her marriage, comforted her when her grandmother died, and counseled her on her Christian ministry.

Cindy got a vision to start a women's ministry at Hope Chapel, but each time she thought of doing it, she was held down by her own list of inadequacies. "I had all the right ideas, suggestions, outlines, etc. I just presented my ideas to the pastor and told him I'd help him look for the right woman to lead the ministry. He said, 'Cindy, you are the right person.' I had never done anything on this scale before, but I called Aunt Cheri, and she encouraged me once again by saying, 'Cindy, I think you know what you have to do.' She was right again. Well, that was almost two years ago, and God has been able to use me (little old me) in a marvelous way, just by my being available and willing."

Cindy's Aunt Cheri has obviously been a strong affirming influence on her life. Are you being an Aunt Cheri or an Aunt Jean to someone you know? Is there someone that comes to your mind right now that might need an encouraging word? I try to keep my eyes and my senses in tune with the Lord's leading, and when he nudges me toward a person, often one I've never seen before, I go.

Cindy concludes her lengthy letter by pledging to be an encourager to others as her aunt has been to her. She hopes to inspire others "to become what my Aunt Cheri has been to me. Her positive reinforcement has had a great impact on my life. I often wonder if I'd have had the strength and confidence to go through these years without her encouraging words. Yes, *words* make the difference!"

Words are powerful whether they are positive or negative. When those words come from a parent or another adult in a position of leadership, they can have a life-changing effect. Raquel's husband and four children are proud that she is finally going back to school to get an AA degree. She says, "My mother never had any words of encouragement. As a result, I didn't graduate from high school." When she told her mother that she was going back to school, her mother's only response was, "It's about time."

Her fifth-grade music teacher told Loree she didn't like her laugh. Loree looks back today at the power those words had on a little eleven-year-old girl. She remembers, "I didn't laugh out loud again until I was fifteen years old."

When Elizabeth was little, her father never helped her with her math homework. She remembers his explaining that since she was a girl, she would never be able to understand it anyway. All through high school and college she only got C's and D's in math. Twenty years later, after much encouragement from her husband, she went back to school and took an algebra class. Elizabeth, the girl who couldn't understand math, got an A!

As a child who never really got to know her father, Christine longed to hear good things from him. Her parents were divorced when she was very young. Dad lived in Texas, and Mom took the kids and moved to California. Mom would give her silver boxes, and then when she went to see "Daddy," not only did he not know how to give out silver boxes, but he seemed especially capable of taking her precious treasures away.

Christine told me, "I became a Christian at nineteen and the Lord began to work in me. I decided to move to Texas, with the excuse of college, to restore the relationship with my father. God did not change him, but He did change me! I loved to give silver boxes, but I felt that I needed them from my dad more than from anyone else. God asked me to let *Him* be my father and accept His silver boxes on behalf of my earthly father. This allowed me to let go of my expectations and my rejections from my earthly father, to love him unconditionally, and to forgive him. My father still loves me conditionally, and yes, sometimes he still knocks my blocks down, but I am learning to offer him silver boxes instead of building a wall and closing him off. I still hope that one day my dad will learn to give a silver box to me."

When Rod was nine years old, he wanted to do something to help out the family's financial situation. He was so proud of himself to have gone out on his own and gotten a paper route. When he bounded into the house to share his good fortune, his excitement quickly faded when, instead of silver boxes, he got comments like: "Do you realize how much time this is going to take? How are you going to get up so early? A young boy like you can't handle that kind of job." Rod was devastated, and he resigned his paper route before ever starting. When he told me the story thirty years later, he commented that he never again shared anything with his parents; he never asked their opinion or discussed decisions with them. There were no silver boxes for Rod.

Loree had three older sisters who were all very talented and pretty. The three sisters were involved in a singing group and were very popular. In their shadow Loree felt ugly, untalented, and unworthy. She felt that she couldn't compare, and she became a very depressed and confused teenager. Nothing anyone could say or do really helped until one day she overheard a conversation between a friend's father and mother. Mr. Clithroe said, "If Loree just felt loved, she would be the prettiest of the four." Loree told me that one comment changed her life.

Kathy Gozur looks back with fond memories on the encouraging words of her father. She says, "He has always been a great Christian role model. Regardless of how ridiculous or crazy my ideas might have been, my father has always given me the encouragement to give it a try. He used to say, 'If you never try, you'll never know.' He felt we should make our own decisions, whether they were right or wrong, good or bad. That way we learned to live with the consequences of our actions. He would tell us, 'If you kids make a bad decision, we as parents will be there for you to help pick up the pieces.' They have always been there regardless of their busy schedules." Every day Kathy's dad gave her little silver boxes with bows on top.

Nothing is more precious to see than a dad who is proud of his offspring. When I attend church with my daughter Marita, I've noticed how Janie Seltzer's dad beams at his daughter who is up in front of the church, the pastor's wife. It is obvious that Jim is proud of his Janie. She remembers as a child calling home while she was away at camp for several weeks. As she told her dad about all the new friends she had made, he gave her a silver box when he said, "Well, of course you have. Everyone wants to be friends with my Janie."

I went out to dinner one night while I was in the midst of writing this book. As I walked into the restaurant in Palm

Springs, two elegant-looking ladies were walking out, and I overheard this conversation:

"My father told me I was a mouse."

"You mean because you are so skinny?"

"No, because he said I have no personality."

"I don't remember him saying that."

The first one emphatically responded, "Well, I sure do!"

Even when I am not looking for them, I find people who are hurting from comments someone else has casually tossed off with little thought to the possible long-range effects.

Remember saying, "I'll never do that! I'll never be like my mother?" Darlene told me that she grew up with a "negative-mouthed mother," and she promised herself that she would never talk to her children as her mother had talked to her. Darlene has worked at being positive with her two boys, but she told me that over the last year or so she has slowly begun to slip in her communication with her oldest who is five and a half. "I was slowly getting negative and saying ugly things just like my mother did. Your message on silver boxes reminded me of how I felt as a child. I am going to put silver boxes in each room to remind me. Thank you!"

Parents often are afraid to give out too many effusive words for fear that their child might get conceited. You may remember hearing someone say, "Be careful or you'll get a big head." Cindy from Manhattan Beach knew she was cute and smart because many people told her so, but her mother didn't. "She never gave me a compliment that I can remember, but she did call me stupid and tell me that I was lazy."

Now at forty years old, Cindy knows intellectually that she is neither stupid nor lazy, but she still struggles with that inbred belief. She told me that her mother's words still overshadow much of what she does and says. "I have believed deep down that I was ugly, though the feedback is that I am rather attractive. Your teaching was fabulous and so good for me. You're a blessing to so many. Much of my life I really have tried subconsciously to prove my mother right. I am working hard to give my husband and my son the silver boxes I never got."

Carolyn is another one who remembers her mother calling her stupid, dumb, and an idiot. She has struggled with any kind of test she had to face. The deep belief that she was stupid kept her from passing most tests the first time. If a job opportunity required a test, Carolyn wouldn't try for it. She even had to take her driving test several times before she passed it. Her mother's words kept her from trying many things throughout her life. Recently Carolyn had to take her driver's test again. For days beforehand she was a nervous wreck, knowing how humiliated she would be by the results. With love and encouragement, her Bible study group prayed for her before and during the driving test. Through God's help Carolyn is beginning to see that her mother's proclamations were wrong. She told me, "I got a perfect score! Can you believe it? I was so thrilled." I could believe it, and a little at a time Carolyn can believe it, too.

Silver boxes do more than just make people feel good. Words have the power to make a person into something or to make him feel like a nothing. Elaine wrote and told me that she loves her parents, but she feels she could have been so much more if her parents had been encouraging instead of discouraging. She proceeded to explain that her mother discouraged whatever she or her brothers and sister did that did not fit her mother's idea of what they should be. Elaine said, "My father was not a discourager, but he also did not encourage. As a result, I grew up stifling my own desires. I grew up and immediately married the first man who asked me. We divorced less than two years later. I subsequently remarried and would not have remained married if it hadn't been for the love and encouragement that I got from my husband's sister and mother. They were a true Christian witness to me. They were my silver boxes!"

Joanne Provost had the potential of being a child who never got any silver boxes. She was strong-willed, aggressive, and opinionated. This type of child is often told things like, "I don't want to hear your voice unless I ask for it! Why don't you ever do things the way I tell you to?" or "You're the problem child." Instead, Joanne's mother gave her silver boxes on a regular basis. She remembers hearing her mother say over and over again, "Joanne, someday you will be a leader!" As others fulfilled their parents' negative prophecies, Joanne fulfilled her mother's positive comments. Joanne told me, "In school I was definitely the leader type. From Christmas plays to recess, I always seemed to be in the lead."

When she left the comfort zone of her Christian elementary school and headed into public high school, she became shy—but only temporarily. "By my senior year, leadership had finally been established, and I was involved in creating a big event at our school. 'Senior Bermuda Day.' My mom's words kept me going, goal after goal after goal." Today Joanne is a teaching director for Community Bible Studies in her area. Throughout all her leadership positions, she has learned one important lesson: "Being a leader does not mean being a boss; it is only possible to lead by being an encourager to others."

Joanne has a five-year-old, strong-willed daughter just like her. She has begun to tell her, "Someday, Katie, you will be a leader for Jesus Christ!"

So many times we mothers who do a decent job of raising our children go to our graves without hearing a silver box of praise: "Well done, good and faithful mother." The Proverbs 31 mother had children who rose up and called her blessed, and some of us have wondered where she found those children. They must have been a different breed in a far-off generation. I was so grateful when Marita volunteered to write the opening and closing chapters in *Raising the Curtain on Raising Children.* In the opening, she tells that our home was not a fairy-tale land full of little angels, but that I had been able to bounce with the punches. In the review chapter, she expressed her feeling that I had done an admirable job as a mother.

"I am so glad that as I was growing up my mother told me I was special and encouraged me. I appreciate all the times she listened to my incessant chatter and my broken dreams. I am thankful for her prayers, for making me what I am today."[4]

Aletha sent me a spontaneous thank-you note her daughter had written to her. I hope it will inspire others of us to write words of appreciation to our mothers.

Dear Mom,

Today I thought of you many times and found a surprising new insight into myself—I suddenly realized just how many things I was able to accomplish and enjoy *today*—all because you cared enough to teach me and show by example over the years. Maybe I am just getting older [31!], but I see now that yes, if we keep at it and not "grow weary in well-doing" a mother can actually influence her child for good—enough to stay with them once they are out from her nest, and even into future generations!

For instance, today I cooked interesting, tasty, and numerous meals—no one ever complains, so I know you taught me well. (I remember your fame among your friends as a great cook.) I sewed today and enjoyed crafting lovely items for my home. (Thank you for reminding me to make it look as good on the inside, too!)

I sat and admired my new living room and marveled at

how much you were able to teach me about color, design, quality, and beauty when you had so little to work with in our home in those tough years that you were a young homemaker. I sang to my children (not nearly as well as you did when we were children) but with joy and enthusiasm nevertheless!

I did several things involving my church—organizing, baking pies, making phone calls, etc. Thank you for a positive Christian home and for yours and Daddy's example of faithfulness even in the small things.

Even as I write this, I realize it is because you also knew how to search for the right words and help them find their way into print. All in all, as Thanksgiving is near, I wish to thank you for all the joy, beauty, and self-confidence you helped me to find in life. And please, always be aware of all the gifts God has given you, and rest assured that you have done your motherly duty well. Be sure that God and your family still have many exciting plans awaiting you. Keep growing. Keep sharing your gifts. Give your love away. I love you very much, and I am

Your grateful daughter.

If you were given silver boxes as a child, it is easy to give them out to others. Elane was the oldest of four, and she says her mom had a storehouse of silver boxes, enough for all of them. Her mother was very creative and encouraged all the children to make and do anything they wanted to do. She remembers her mother's greatest gift to her was the ability to see her mistakes in a positive light, not as failures.

"When we would mess up our drawings, she would say, 'That's not a mistake; let's just make it into a flower—see now your painting looks great!' My paintings were full of clouds, flowers, and trees that were there to cover a slipped pen. I am now an art teacher, and I teach like my mother. My children's projects are full of clouds and flowers. My mom changed my picture of myself and has made my life into something beautiful. It has only been in the last year that I realized what a perfect picture of Romans 8:28 she gave us. How many of my bad choices in life has God changed and worked into flowers later on." Elane has many silver boxes full of flowers—flower boxes.

"See! The winter is past; the rains are over and gone. Flowers appear on the earth; the season of singing has come" (Song of Songs 2:11–12, NIV).

8

School Boxes

*N*ext to family members, teachers have the greatest influence on the lives of children. I remember how I looked up to my teachers and wanted so much to hear an encouraging word. I remember Miss McCormick, fresh out of college herself, who told me I could learn Latin and I would be glad later that I understood the roots, prefixes, and suffixes of English words that were derivatives of Latin. She was right. She challenged us beyond our self-perceived ability, she had us conversing in Latin sentences, and she gave us a rich background in vocabulary that I still depend upon today.

I also remember my geology professor who saw me lean over and whisper to a friend, and chose to make an example of me before the whole class. I'll never forget the humiliation as I had to stand before the full lecture hall and recite ten times, "A mountain is an extreme example of diastrophism."

I remember tall, elegant elderly Miss Croston who taught us never to say, "I don't think so." Instead, we were to say, "I think not." She would say, "Never let anyone know you don't think. They will find it out soon enough." To this day if I catch myself saying "I don't think so," I hear Miss Croston's words in my ear.

When I look back to grammar school and the little school boxes we carried with our pencils, ruler, and eraser, I remember how we brought notes home from our teachers in our boxes. Some notes were notices of meetings, some were words of affirmation, and a few said, "Florence talks too much." Whether they were good or bad, these slips of paper came home in our school boxes—and some lived there for days before we dared to pull them out and show them to our parents.

As I have shared the value of encouraging words in the silver box message, stories about teachers have poured in showing the great influence a teacher can have in the life of a child.

Esther Pearson, a marriage and family counselor, remembers an experience that affected her life. In eighth grade, she tried very hard to get a B in her favorite subject, history. She did extra work and was sure she had surpassed anything she had ever achieved. When her report card came, she got all C's. She mustered up every bit of strength she could to face this teacher and courageously say, "There must be a mistake." Without any thought as to how his comment would be received, he answered, "No, Esther, there's no mistake. You are a C student and that's that." Esther felt defeated and quit trying to be any better than a C student. It wasn't until she was twenty-six that she realized she could actually get A's if she put forth enough effort, but as she says, "Much had been lost."

Teachers play an important part in helping children feel good about themselves. A simple comment from a person of position can give little ones the confidence that they can do something. Mrs. Harmon was one of those teachers whom students laughed about in the restrooms. She was a sickly little woman with dyed black hair, and she "had the aroma of a perfume factory." Despite these features, Mrs. Harmon saw something good in each of her students and encouraged them in their unique abilities.

Margaret Begly remembers looking back through her high-school yearbook just before her twentieth class reunion. There on the faculty page was a forgotten silver box from Mrs. Harmon. Margaret told me, "I remember being a real stinker as a student, but Mrs. Harmon saw something in me I didn't see or believe. The note she wrote expressed her admiration for me: 'You have a magnetic personality. You are a joy to me, and I know you will go far in life.'" It has taken Margaret years to be able to believe Mrs. Harmon's words, but in rereading them she was truly encouraged by that little silver box from many years ago.

Leanne Williams told me about a sixth-grade teacher who really turned her life around. Leanne felt that she was average, at best, or maybe even below average. Her teacher encouraged her to give her studies her all. Even though she didn't excel, when it was time for Honors Assembly, the teacher placed Leanne in the seating for the honors students although she wasn't actually one of them. Through this teacher's encouragement and her willingness to take a chance on Leanne by placing her above her level and expecting her to reach it, this young girl stretched beyond herself and got straight A's from then on.

Debbie Heavilin remembers a teacher's comment that made a big impact on her life, a silver box which she has been able to keep with her and polish on a regular basis. "I was an average student in English. My teacher could have criticized my work, but instead she said, 'I admire you because you work well under pressure.' Ever since then when the pressure mounts, I remember what she said, and it helps give me strength to tackle the problem I am facing." Isn't it amazing that one simple sentence can have such an impact on a person's life?

Little ones need lots of hugs and kisses. If they don't get those kinds of silver boxes at home, they often head off to school where they are fidgety and agitate others as a way to get that needed attention. Mrs. Bell, Bonnie Ramirez's second-grade teacher, had a solution for that problem as she showed each one how much she loved them. Bonnie recalls, "She was my silver box with a bow on top because every morning when I arrived in her class she would give me a hug and a kiss."

Imagine the excitement of a fifteen-year-old girl who is going to the beach with her church youth group for the first time. That excitement is doubled when she has been invited to accompany the most popular boy in church. Carol Hulin was that girl. Shy and ordinary in her own eyes, Carol could hardly wait for the big day. Finally it came. She got ready and went to the church to join the others. One by one the others came, gathered up their belongings and loaded into the bus. There stood Carol, still waiting for Greg to show up. It was time to leave and she was still alone. The youth leader came over and said, "Carol, the loss is totally Greg's—he has missed out on a very special privilege to be with you." One simple sentence changed Carol from feeling stupid to feeling special and gave her a desperately needed silver box that she has never misplaced.

While one little comment can lift up a person's life, the wrong words can also ruin one. Barbara Aro has horrible memories of three years in junior high school. The stage was set the very first week. She had forgotten to bring her book home the night before, and therefore she hadn't done her homework for Mrs. McKinley's English class. Barbara wrote me, "I was terrified of the consequences! I was doing the work in class when I was called upon to give the next answer.

I gave a wrong answer to a question that the teacher thought was easy. Mrs. McKinley replied, 'Good grief, you're dumb!' The whole class laughed at me." Barbara was having a hard time making friends at this new school, and now it was impossible. She begged her mother to let her go to another school, but she made her stay to learn to adjust to adverse circumstances. Barb was nicknamed the "Good grief, you're dumb kid" and built up a lot of resentment as she suffered through those three years.

It took Candy twelve years to realize that she did have what it took to go to college. She wanted to go right after high school, but the comments of her parents and teachers discouraged her. "They told me I should be a professional cheerleader because I was such an airhead. I believed it and didn't realize they were wrong until I was twenty-eight years old and my husband encouraged me to go back to school."

Terri Geary went to a Christian high school where she decided to take what was called the commercial course. The principal had wanted Terri to pursue nursing or teaching, both areas that Terri had no interest in and no aptitude for. Terri enjoyed typing, shorthand, writing letters, and the other things that went with an office environment. When she told the principal what she had decided, the woman's response was: "I'm sorry. I didn't realize that you would want to take the easy way out of high school." Terri felt that she had made the right choice for her life, but the comment of a person in a position of respect made her feel totally worthless.

"I've never forgotten how small, how insignificant, how dumb I felt when she said that—how useless she made me feel my life would be."

I'm sure the principal meant to challenge Terri to what she thought was a better choice, but instead she wiped out her initiative.

Whether we are teachers or parents, let's try to stuff those school boxes with notes of praise.

"O God, thou hast taught me from my youth: and hitherto have I declared thy wondrous works" (Psalm 71:17).

9

Stolen Boxes

*B*arry, an enthusiastic young Christian, went to a course on evangelism so he would be a more effective witness. Near the conclusion of the course, he and one of the instructors went out for some door-to-door witnessing as a sort of final exam. They knocked on the first door. A man was home and invited them in. After a lengthy presentation with positive results and a promise to attend their church the following Sunday, Barry left with his silver box firmly under his arm. Before he ever had a chance to polish his box, however, it was knocked from his grip when his instructor gave the report card. "I have heard the gospel presented 252 times and presented it 67 times myself. That was the worst presentation I've ever heard." With this instructor as head of evangelism, it is no surprise that the church has trouble getting members out for witnessing night.

Now that we understand the value of a positive word, we need to ask ourselves: are we giving out silver boxes or are we dropping words on certain people under certain circumstances that would not be considered a gift? James says, "We all stumble in many ways. If anyone is never at fault in what he says, he is a perfect man, able to keep his whole body in check" (James 3:2, NIV).

Chances are there are few of us who have our tongues under perfect control and who never give out a negative word. Think for a moment about the people you've talked with in the past few days. Make a mental list of those to whom you gave uplifting words, those people who make you smile when you think of them, those who agree with you and please you, those who bring out the best in you. Who are they? Are they family or friends?

Now think of those whose mere presence in the room is enough to set your teeth on edge. People who never have a kind word to say to you. People who look down upon you and make you feel insecure. People who seldom, if ever, agree with you with any degree of enthusiasm. Who are they?

If they are people whom you could avoid, people whom you've forced yourself to tolerate due to some misplaced sense of martyrdom, perhaps you could make an effort to stay out of their destructive path. Sometimes a mate takes a sly sadistic pleasure out of insisting we spend time with someone who drains the very energy out of us. If this is the case, explain to your spouse that when you are pulled down by this person's problems you have very little strength left to be loving and affirming to your family. Being in the presence of negative people any more than we have to is asking for trouble.

If you can detach yourself from any sense of responsibility for these people's programmed pessimism about life and about you—and realize it's not your fault that they haven't had a happy day in years—then perhaps you can develop an objective sense of humor about the situation. It's always easier to laugh when you're not involved, but often when you stop taking comments to heart and back up a little to get a more balanced perspective, you can at least smile.

Our friend Jim sent me a letter he had received from his cousin. This relative had appeared at Jim's mother's funeral with her camera. At Christmas Jim, who was still grieving over the loss of his mother, received a letter from the cousin enclosing pictures of his mother in the casket taken from all different angles. If the pictures weren't enough to unnerve him for the day, she sent the following words—hardly silver boxes.

> I'm sorry I haven't written sooner. You see, my husband's father is dying of cancer and has moved in with us. Our youngest daughter's mother-in-law has only a few weeks to live, and I have had to keep her [the daughter's] children while she sits at the hospital. Our oldest daughter was attacked in Washington, D.C., last month and is in

rather serious condition in the hospital. I have been fighting with depression for some time and don't know if I will ever get over it.

I hope this letter serves to cheer you up during this holiday season—I know how much you must miss your mom. If you ever get back to West Virginia, please look me up. . . .

Would you want to look up that dear cousin? Not on your life!

Jim wrote, "There is no way I want to go within fifty miles of that lady! I'm certain I would get cancer, Sherri would be mugged, someone near me would die of some terminal illness, and my children would go through extreme depression. . . . I swear to you I am not stretching the truth!"

Isn't it amazing how an objective view on a situation can often give the relief of a little chuckle, a breath of cleansing air?

If you can't avoid the person, disentangle your emotions, or find the humor in the relationship, what can you do? Two things simultaneously: First, start praying, not that God will change or kill off the offender, but that he will change *your* attitude—or at least your tolerance level. God doesn't necessarily work well second-hand on that other person according to your will, but it's amazing how quickly he responds when you ask for a change of heart for yourself. In praying for the ability to love the unlovely, your responsibility is to be open to God's power and purpose. You can't say, "Make me understand, love, or forgive Uncle Charlie" and then underneath be thinking, *But I'll hate him till my dying day.*

In addition to prayer for a change of heart, whether or not this person deserves it, the second thing you can do is to start giving some positive strokes to this offending friend whether or not he acknowledges receipt of the card, note, or gift. In spiritual terms, which are opposite of human nature, our responsibility ceases when we have done the right thing, and we don't need to hear praises or thank-yous. Once we've made the positive word or gesture, the responsibility lies in the other person's court.

Humanly speaking we want credit and thanks for what we've done, but in God's sight the selfless act itself is what's important. We may do good deeds and say good words and never get response, but we know at least we've done our part toward restoration, and it's up to God to change the other person's heart in his time.

I have one friend who has an extremely difficult in-law. For Christmas my friend sent this in-law a certificate for a once-a-month delivery of high-quality fresh fruit. After a few months of these gifts, the response was, "I'm sick of getting this fruit. I don't like it anyway. Tell them to stop sending it."

For those of us who would love such a gift, this reaction is unbelievable. But coming from a negative person who is determined to see no good, it is a natural part of their miserable outlook on life. Our responsibility ends with the kind gesture; our compassion begins with their rejection of our gifts.

What if you find you are saying unkind words to someone you really love, someone who is not negative or offensive but who just seems to bring out the worst in you. Is there someone like that in your life—a mate, a son, a daughter? Ask yourself two questions: First, is there some cause from my background that makes me respond poorly to this family member? Did my father or mother say similar things to me? Was there some trauma in my childhood that this person somehow triggers memories of? Is there a subconscious retaliation for what was done or said?

If these questions bring up any response in you, I think you will find our book *Freeing Your Mind from Memories That Bind* helpful. When we have suffered some childhood rejection or abuse, our reactions often come from the depths of that pain. And just trying to modify our behavior and be nice doesn't seem to work. In *Freeing Your Mind from Memories That Bind*, we have laid out for you questions that will lead you to the source of your problems so that you can heal from the inside out and not continue to stick on Christian Band-Aids that fall off when the mental resolve begins to fail.

The second question to ask yourself is this: Does this loved one not seem to appreciate you as much as others do? Does he look bored when you talk or pass by without speaking? Does she not notice your new clothes or not appear to give you the time of day? Most of us have little trouble relating to those who obviously love us and tell us so, or to those who appreciate our every word and respond to our humor, or to those who praise us and worship the ground we walk on. They give us silver boxes, and we make every day Christmas for them.

But thrown into every family is that one who doesn't press our happy button—one who, frankly, turns us off. As fine Christian people, we don't like to admit that we don't really love everyone unconditionally. We like to feel it's that other person's fault. If only he or she would change. Once we stop wishing on a star, however, and admit we're part of the problem, God begins to do a healing work in our hearts.

As I look back over raising my children, I realize how easy it was to give silver boxes to Lauren. Right from the beginning, she behaved well. She was mature and responsible with the babies, she got good marks, was a cheerleader, and came in on time at night. She liked me to be involved as a room-mother, and she knew she could use our home for parties or Bible studies and as a haven for troubled friends. She thanked me for what I did, and I appreciated her for what she was.

Marita didn't fit the good, dutiful child mold, but whatever she did was fun. I'd go to punish her, and she'd come out with a line so hilarious that I'd start to laugh. She always knew how to win me over. Even though I knew I was being conned, the process was so enjoyable I didn't mind.

Until I understood the four basic personality patterns, I didn't understand our son Fred. I wondered why he was so quiet and why he didn't respond to the high energy level of our household. Underneath I guess I was a little hurt that he didn't think I was funny. I remember well the day when, as a teenager, he said to me, "It amazes me that people pay money to hear you talk." As I stood silent and speechless by the stove, he continued, "I guess that's because they don't have to listen to you for nothing." He sighed and walked off, leaving me without an answer. Where could I go with that evaluation of my lifetime career?

In retrospect, I know that Fred wasn't condemning my speaking or me personally. As a teen, he was just becoming aware of what I did, and he was frankly amazed that his ordinary mother's words were of value. He was only expressing what had come to his mind at the moment, and he never mentioned it again. Consciously, I put the comment aside, but somewhere up in the ledger of my mind I have a tiny column labeled "slights and hurts," and I must have put a faint check mark beside Fred's name.

Not long after that incident, Fred came home one afternoon and cheerfully said, "Mrs. Johnson told me that I have a charming personality." Without even thinking, I retorted, "I'd sure like to see some of that charm around here." After I'd let that statement loose and seen the crushed look on his face, I began to wonder where those words had come from. What made a loving mother toss off an unkind and unnecessary comment to a good boy who was enthused over a compliment he'd received? Was it that column in my head where I had checked off a hurt and was subconsciously waiting to get even? How difficult it is for us as parents to admit that we do keep score, that we do remember what we perceive as a negative.

In retrospect, I realize that Mrs. Johnson had given Fred a big silver box which he'd brought proudly home. I could have given him another one, but instead I grabbed Mrs. Johnson's box and threw it away. I left him to go to his room empty-handed.

Do you have some empty-handed people in your home? Some children who are desperate for a kind word and you're not giving them any? A mate who's afraid to tell you of a compliment for fear you'll say, "Well, they should try living with you!" Is there anyone whom you really love that wouldn't dare show you their silver box because they know you'd smash it, kick it, or throw it in the trash?

How I wish I could redeem some of my family's silver boxes that have been reduced to rubbish in one way or another. How I wish I could find them, freshen up the silver paper, and put a new bow on top.

My example of taking the box away from my son has brought many letters with a similar theme. Mary came to a retreat where I spoke on Silver Boxes. The night before, she had been sharing with her friends that she had difficulty handling her five-year-old John Richard. Others had brought up some of their struggles also and encouraged each other with their victories. On Sunday when I was speaking and told about my response to Fred's "charming personality" line, Mary's friend leaned over and said, "Poor John Richard," meaning the poor child was in for a rough life with her for a mother. Those three words devastated Mary, and she wrote me, "I felt my blocks come smashing to the floor, and I started to cry. In fact I had to leave the room because I was hurting so badly. Boy, did your words ring true to me. Words can kill."

One minute we can be on cloud nine. Moments later, after a few words are spoken, we may feel worthless and insignificant. The silver box can be snatched away quicker than we have time to say thank you to the giver. The pain is deeper when the person who unties the bow is someone that we look up to, respect, or admire. When it is Mom who steals our box, we can end up feeling like plain brown wrapping looking for the glow of the silver paper for the rest of our lives.

Greta told me about a special silver box her sister gave her as a graduation present. "My gift from my sister was an appointment at the beauty salon to have my hair cut in the latest style, a short shingled cut. After it was done, I thought I looked great and could hardly wait to show my family. They were eating dinner when I arrived. I asked, 'How do you like my new hair cut?' My mother looked at me and said, 'Well, if you ever had any beauty, you've lost it all now!'" Greta was deflated and hurt. She had never felt loved and now this proved it. All her life she longed for a silver box from her mother, something to make her shine, something to make her feel special. Finally, in her mother's dying days, at eighty-three years old, her mother told Greta that she loved her.

Becky says she doesn't tell jokes well. People used to laugh at her funny stories, but one comment from her mother made her think they were laughing *at* her, not with her. Twenty years later, she still remembers entertaining the family at a reunion. After she finished telling a funny story, her mother criticized her for not enunciating and for smiling too much while she talked. Becky said, "It was a minor comment on her part, but it immediately made me think 'Oh no, I embarrassed myself. I was stupid. Everybody was laughing at me.'"

It has taken Becky's husband ten years to build her self-esteem back up. When they first met, he told her that she was pretty, a good worker, capable, bright, and creative. She says, "Ten years later he's still telling me. Ten years later I'm beginning to agree with him." When a silver box has been taken away, it takes a lot more of them to fill the void that was left behind. Thank God Becky's husband loved her enough to keep dropping boxes into what must have seemed like a bottomless pit.

As a senior in high school, Martha was the best typist in her school. She was sent to a state typing contest. With her manual typewriter, she typed an amazing 112 words a minute with no mistakes. She came in second. Another student with an electric typewriter typed six more words than she did. Martha remembers being happy with second place. Upon proudly presenting her second place trophy to her mother, Martha was told, "You could have won if you weren't so lazy." Less than ten words were spoken, but Martha has never typed again.

Mothers who mean well often give a silver box to their children, and then through some quirk in their maternal wisdom take it back with the very next breath. For some it is almost like breathing. They breathe out and give a silver box. They breathe in and take it away, leaving their child with their empty hands outstretched. Even if the child is now an adult, moms feel that it is their place to continue correction.

Since coming in contact with the silver box story, Wanda Mishler has begun to notice that she is one of those who gives but takes away. Wanda told me about her son's first sermon. When he was finished preaching, she told him how good it was. In the next breath, she said, "But you didn't give the scripture you said we should look up."

Wanda went on to tell me, "When he saw his wife, he said 'I told you my mom would do it. She gave me the silver box, and then took it away.' Then he told his wife what I had said. Bless her heart, she came and told me, and I am trying hard to change."

While Pam has positive memories of her beauty pageant victory, the silver box was bittersweet. She remembers that her win was especially exciting to her family. Because of their uneducated, lower class background, her win gave them recognition in the community. After the pageant the entire family was on stage basking in the moment. Pam's stepsister and her beautiful baby boy were there, too. (The stepsister had married at sixteen and had a baby eleven months later.) The joy of Pam's special moment was shattered when her stepfather turned to her stepsister and said, "Why couldn't you have done something good like this?" Pam still has the silver box in the form of a trophy, but its shine is tarnished. And although the comment didn't come from Pam, it ruined the relationship of these sisters.

Martha remembers one time shopping with her mother when she was fourteen. A saleslady gave her a silver box with a beautiful bow on top. The saleslady admired how pretty she was in the dress she had on and suggested that she should be a teen model. She gave Martha the name of the person in the store to see about modeling. When their shopping was finished, Martha excitedly asked her mother, "Could we go to the office now?" Her bubble was burst by her mother's response, "Oh, Martha, she was just saying that to make a sale."

LeAnne had a teacher in eighth grade that made her feel special. He offered anyone in the entire class a free lunch in the school cafeteria if they got straight A's in his basic education class. LeAnne remembers working very hard to get the A's, and when report card time came, she had straight A's and got her free lunch. She continued diligently in his class and got a free lunch every report period until she told her mother about it. The motivation to succeed was stolen from her when her mother forbade her to ever have lunch with the teacher again. LeAnne told me, "From then on I had nothing to work toward—I had no goal."

Alyson was the first girl in her high school to be elected as student body president. In her excitement, she rushed to the phone to call her mother and tell her the good news. Upon hearing of her daughter's triumph, the mother responded with, "Don't let it go to your head." The joy of Alyson's silver box was quickly snatched away.

Dear Florence,

I really enjoyed your lecture today on "Little Silver Boxes." It points out someone I should be nicer to. Also, I can't help wondering, is there any way to keep people from taking away a "silver box" that you just got from someone else?

Thanks again!
Vicki (15 years old)

Can you put a new bow on top of an old box? Can you fluff up the tattered ribbon and push out the dents of damaging words?

We've all heard the example of a pillow that is ripped open and the feathers float far and wide, never to be retrieved and stuffed back into the ticking again. Our words are like those feathers. We can never get them back. Once we've let one loose, we can't catch it. Much as we might want to, we cannot eat our words.

Should we then give up? Say there's no hope? Cry woe is me? Put on sackcloth and ashes? Light candles? Do penance?

The first step is to realize that we are smashing more silver boxes than we are giving out. Awareness of the problem is a good beginning.

Next, we have to prayerfully search our memories for any checkmarks we have been scoring against other people. Do this research project quietly by yourself, and write down everything that comes to mind. Don't shut off the flow saying to yourself, "Well, I really didn't mean that the way it sounded." Write it down. If you can't come up with anything you've said that was hurtful or find any grudges you're holding toward others, then you and your friends are either perfect or in extreme denial.

Once you allow these repressed thoughts, scores, or comments to the surface, you'll be amazed at how fast you can get rid of them. Bring them to the Lord and say, "Lord, I didn't realize I'd been keeping track of every unkind word anyone ever gave me. I didn't know that I tried to even up the score by saying nasty things back to those who hurt me. Wipe my slate clean on both sides and give me the will to hand out silver boxes to my family and friends."

Sue's daughter Emily was seven years old when her teacher praised her regularly for her good behavior. One day when Sue went to the school to pick Emily up, the teacher gave Emily a silver box. The teacher said, "Emily is so good, she could be citizen of the month every month!" Sue observed, "I quickly took the box away when I gasped, 'Are we talking about the same child?' It seemed that Emily was happy and pleasant while she was away from us and saved up all her 'ugliness' for the family."

Sue continues, "Emily recently brought home a progress report with a teacher's note, 'I really enjoy Emily's sweet, pleasant personality.' This time I was determined not to steal my seven-year-old's silver box. We made a big deal over the comment and really praised her. It has been several weeks since this report, and we have rarely seen ugly behavior since."

Is it possible to rebuild relationships? Can we put a new bow on old paper?

In June of 1984, I was scheduled to go on a trip to Europe and the Holy Land. The churches sponsoring the trip asked me to go along, speak on the personalities, and counsel those who had needs. They told me I could bring one other person with me. As long as I paid the airfare, they would cover the food and lodging. Naturally, I asked my husband, but he could not take three weeks out of the office at that time. I thought of Lauren. With all her energy, we would charge through Europe and not miss a thing. We'd walk through each museum, cover each cathedral and climb to the top of each turret and tower. But Lauren had two little ones she couldn't leave for all that time.

My mind jumped to Marita. Oh, what fun we would have. We could laugh our way through Europe. She has the knack of seeing the hilarious in any situation. But Marita had only been married a short while, and I couldn't pull her away for three weeks. I then thought of young Fred, but I knew he wouldn't want to go. I remember praying, "Lord, should I ask Fred? He doesn't even enjoy my company. How could he stand being with me for three weeks—sitting next to each other on the planes, trains, and buses, and sharing the same room every night?"

I presented the possibility to my son and he became enthused over the trip. As we prepared to go, I prayed that I would have a positive attitude, that I would not push him into activities he disliked, that I would adjust to his personality and not expect him to change for me. I realized that I was the adult, I had the knowledge of the personalities, and I had the wisdom to modify my ways and accept his.

My husband met with young Fred and explained that he was to be in charge of the tickets and the money. He was to help me with the arrangements of the different rooms where I would be speaking. He was to see that the bags were packed and out on time each day. And he was to "take care of his mother."

Fred did all he was assigned to do and more. While he changed the money as we entered each new country, I held back, let him do it, and didn't double-check to see if it was right. During those three weeks, our relationship went from controlling mother with little son to an adult male caring for the needs of his mother. We became friends.

The trip was not automatic bliss, however, because of the difference in our personalities. My strong nature wanted to see everything there was to see, whereas his melancholy mind wanted to sit quietly and reflect. We'd get to a stop and the guide would announce, "We're going to tour another cathedral."

I'd say, "Get up Fred; we're going to tour another cathedral."

He'd respond, "I don't want to see another cathedral."

In the past I would have said, "I didn't ask you if you wanted to see another cathedral. I told you to get up off your seat and march through that cathedral. Don't you realize how much money it cost me to bring you over here, and the more cathedrals you march through, the cheaper it is per capita per cathedral for me?"

Fortunately, I didn't say that. Instead, I let him stay in the bus and brought him back brochures. I found out on that trip that my son enjoys looking at the ceiling of a bus as much as the ceiling of the Sistine Chapel.

When we were going through the Alps, I woke him up and said, "Look out the window, Fred; these are the Alps." He opened his eyes, looked out the right side of the bus, across the front, down the left side, and then shut his eyes. I couldn't believe he didn't get excited, and I repeated "These are the ALPS!" He answered, "I know. I just saw them." With my son, if you've seen one Alp you've seen them all!

On the day we passed from Jordan into Israel, the temperature was extremely high. Going through the checkpoint involved a long procedure of searching through luggage and examining passports with armed soldiers standing guard. The heat in the parked bus was stifling. We got out and leaned against the front of an army truck that was nearby. I felt sick, and as I thought about how uncomfortable I was, I began to faint. I slid slowly down the grill of the truck toward the rocky road. Fred said later that I kept getting shorter and shorter. He grabbed me and pulled me up, and I came to without ever having hit the ground. He led me into the bus, laid me out across the back seat, and fanned me until our bus was allowed to proceed and a little air came in through the open windows.

There was a young girl on our tour who loved taking pictures of me in ungainly positions. She didn't give me time to do a pivot turn and strike a pose. She got me leaning over water coolers from the rear. One day she approached and said, "Your son really loves you." I was delighted and could hardly wait for the list of my motherly virtues that she was about to share. Instead she said, "Yesterday you fell asleep on the bus. Your head was against the window, your mouth was open, and you looked real funny." I already didn't like this story, but she went on anyway. "I was sitting across the aisle, and I decided to take a picture of you looking strange like that. I focused my camera on you and just as I was about to take the picture, your son moved his whole body in front of you. I asked what he was doing and he asked what I was doing. I told him, 'I'm going to take a picture of your mother looking funny like that.' He stared at me and said, 'You will take no more pictures of my mother without asking her permission first.'" She then softened her voice and concluded, "Your son really loves you."

Her story wasn't quite what I'd expected, but what a wonderful thing I learned—when the chips are down, my boy is on my side.

The last night of our trip, young Fred and I were standing on the balcony of the Jerusalem Hilton looking out at this ancient city with its bright lights and quaint buildings. As we stood there quietly, I wondered what the trip would have been like if Lauren had been along. We'd no doubt be out racing through the narrow streets and alleys making sure we hadn't missed anything. If Marita had been with me, we'd probably be laughing about the places and the people, but Fred and I were just standing. After what seemed like a long time of silence to me, Fred spoke up and said, "Mother, this has been the best trip of my life."

"It has? Why?"

"Because it's been so quiet and you haven't made me talk. I've had time to think and develop my philosophy of life."

I didn't know he knew what a philosophy was, and all this time he'd been developing one!

I praise God for what he taught us both on that trip. We got to know each other as friends, and I learned that whether I faint or fall asleep, my son will watch over me.

After hearing me speak on the Silver Boxes, eighty-one-year-old Evelyn Doyle went home and got out this poem she had written. She sent it to me so that I would enjoy it and let others read it, too.

VERBOSITY

My mouth runneth over—
A problem with which long I've coped—
When humility, justice, kindness and love,
Are traits for which I'd hoped.

Something within me starts to churn,
When any subject at all comes up.
For the life of me, I cannot just sit,
And quietly hold my cup.

There are other cups to fill—
So I jump in both feet first,
With very little persuasion—
Just the first pause that occurs.

I extract, examine, explain and exhort—
You might say monopolize—
Till the Lord in His Mercy shows me
Interest waning in my listener's eyes.

Verbosity can be a gift—or a curse—
Can make one a star—or a bore—
Depending upon who is coaching one
And the richness of one's lore.

Deep down inside I'd rather not be
One with the verbal skill—
To slay dragons—feed impossible dreams—
Or spew words with power to kill.

So each day must start with meditation
And for guidance a petition
If speak I must, and I must speak—
Let my words be those of blessing.

—Evelyn Meyer Doyle

"Set a watch, O Lord, before my mouth; keep the door of my lips" (Psalm 141:3).

10

Special Boxes

*I*n Paul's letters to Timothy, Paul gives Timothy words of encouragement and calls him "son"—a way of showing how special he was to him. The dictionary tells us that a special person is one who is unique, individual, one-of-a-kind, extraordinary, and of great significance. Wouldn't we all like to be special, of great significance in the eyes of at least one person?

When I teach about how special Timothy was to Paul, the reaction varies. Those who know they were special to someone as they were growing up become positively sentimental; those who have never felt special in the eyes of anyone seem sad and sometimes cry. What an opportunity all of us have available to make others feel special. Whether it is our mate, a parent, a child, a grandchild, someone at church or at work, what a blessing we could be to others if we made them feel special.

Bill Garrity came to our "Meeting of the Men" where he heard Fred and Bob Barnes both mention doing special things for your wife that would surprise her and not let your marriage settle into a dull drab existence. During the two-hour Saturday afternoon break, Bill went out to the shopping mall and bought streamers, red hearts, flowers, balloons, and Anna's favorite candy. He hung the streamers across the hotel room, taped hearts on the mirrors, put flowers on every table and floated balloons in the corners. He laid out Anna's favorite candy with a romantic card beside it. Because seventeen years ago he had given Anna her engagement ring inside a Cracker Jack box, he also bought her a box of Cracker Jacks for a touch of humor. When Anna arrived at the hotel Saturday evening in time for the banquet, Bill greeted her with a room full of surprises. When Anna told me this story, she was in tears—tears of joy.

"He could have spent the afternoon relaxing with the other men or taking a nap, but instead he took his time to decorate the room and give me a lift after a long day's work."

After I'd talked to both Anna and Bill about their unusual time together in the hotel, she said, "Of all the things he's ever done, this was the most fun. It was a silver box with a bow on top."

So many people have told me of the encouragement they continually get from rereading written notes, I was delighted when Monica Wooff gave me her example.

Born and raised in South Africa in a Christian home, she grew up with very affirming parents who always made her feel special. Her Sanguine mother made the home fun and always had an appropriate saying for every situation. Monica wrote:

> It's funny how all the little sayings you hear in your child-hood seem to stay with you. I always thought my mom was so clever because she had a pocketful of smart things to say for everything. It was only as I grew older that I realized she was using Scripture. They all came from the book of Proverbs. As I've raised my children, I've been amazed at how easily the appropriate Proverb that my mom said so many times comes to my mind.

Monica's mother gave her silver boxes that she automatically passes on to others. Imagine how difficult it was for Monica when she and her husband left the warm support of their families in South Africa and moved to California eleven years ago. At first, she was terribly lonely without the encouraging words she was used to receiving. Within a short period of time, however, she found a church home that had many hurting people in it. They were in need of counsel, so she became busy helping and encouraging others. Because she always had a word of cheer, people assumed she had no needs of her own. Her ministry was all giving and no receiving. One day when she was feeling drained from constant counseling, a note of thanks arrived in her mailbox. This cheered her so much that she kept it and read it over often. Soon other cards and notes appeared with special words of encouragement to her. Monica writes:

> Soon I had a stack of these notes, so I decided to cover some shoe boxes with pretty paper because I thought such special cards needed to be kept in an attractive box. Now on days when I am down and need some encouragement or just want to stroll down memory lane with some loved ones, I pull out one of my treasure chests and take a handful of cards and read them. I laugh and cry, but somehow I feel touched and loved by one of God's children, and my needs are met.

What a unique idea to keep a growing collection of silver boxes in a group of treasure chests.

Paula Allaire wrote of her need to feel special. "Silver boxes were very rare from my mother. As a child, I would silently beg her in my heart to please speak to me, please touch me. That word or touch never seemed to come.

"As an adult, in the past few years, I have received special, unexpected notes that really touched and encouraged me. I wanted to keep these notes close, to be reread when I needed them. I put them in my Bible which goes everywhere with me, but they kept dropping out. Because I was afraid that I would lose those "special words" that I so much needed, I took a five-by-seven-inch manila clasp envelope in which I placed my special notes, and I glued it in the back of my Bible. Now whenever I need a silver box, I open my Bible and they are there waiting for me, ready to lift me up and help me to go forward again."

This past Christmas I got special notebooks for each of my three grandsons. I put pocket pages in the front of each notebook as a place for them to save the cards and notes I send them. I also wrote a letter to each one telling them the feelings I had when I first saw them a few moments after their births. I described how they looked; and in Jonathan's case, I told of all the mishaps of my day in trying to get to the hospital before he was born. (Although those mishaps were not pleasant at the time, in retrospect, they are humorous.)

I have also included personal stories about them that have to do with my very special times with them. Each essay is full of silver boxes of praise for them to read whenever their self-worth needs a boost. Jonathan asks me, "Grammie, would you read your book about me?" Little Bryan, only three, takes me by the hand and shows me his special book. He opens the cover and points to the picture of me holding him as a newborn. "That's you and me when I was a little tiny baby."

For those of you grandparents who want to make sure your little ones save the encouraging words you mail them, provide them with a treasure chest, a manila envelope, or a scrapbook that will become an automatic home for their memories. When they get discouraged and their skies are cloudy all day, they will know where to reach to pull out their own personal silver box.

From the beginning I have called my first grandchild, Randy, my special boy. He knows that his Grammie loves him. When he was in kindergarten, I went to pick him up one day, and his teacher asked if he'd like to introduce me. He took me by the hand, led me over to the children in a circle on the floor and said, "This is my Grammie, and I'm her special boy."

What a blessing his comment was to me—and how glad I am that Randy knows he's special. As I have received so many stories about children who were not encouraged by anyone, I know how important it is for us grandparents to give positive words to these little ones.

Randy has beautiful skin that tans easily. I often stroke his cheek and comment, "Your skin is like velvet." One day his teacher had each child fill out a self-inventory. On the question, "What do you like best about yourself?" Randy wrote, "My skin." The teacher had never received such an answer. When my daughter told me this, I realized how important it is to affirm our little ones in every way we can, for when Randy was asked this question, the first thing that came to his mind was my constant comment that his skin is like velvet.

What would a child write who didn't know he had soft skin, or bright eyes, or pretty hair? What does a child think about himself when he's never felt special in any way?

When Judi Resha's son Scott was in preschool, he was smaller than all the other children. They all teased him about his size: "You're too little to be with us. Why are you in this room—you must be just one year old." The teacher saw the hurt look on his face, and in front of the other children she said, "Scott is the most kind and loving boy in our class, and I want you all to know that special things come in small packages." Judi heard this positive statement and watched as the other children smiled with acceptance. As he has gone up through the grades, Scott has often been taunted about his size, and he is able to respond, "Special things come in small packages." What a blessing this teacher was to Scott by turning a negative situation into a positive one and making him feel special.

Bonnie wrote me that on her first day in first grade, her mother spanked her in front of the whole class. She can't remember why; she just remembers how she felt. She was sure everyone hated her, and she was deeply embarrassed. Her teacher reached out to comfort her, and the next day the teacher had a tea party for just the two of them. Bonnie wrote:

> She showed me that I was special to her. This went on for a week. The rest of the class envied our tea party. After a week, she encouraged me to invite another classmate to our party. Each day we invited more to our party until the whole class was included. The tea parties dissolved, and I became friends with everyone and gained confidence. Today I teach fourth grade, and I try to make each child feel special.

Diana Williams looks back upon her childhood and sees a neglected little girl with a melancholy personality and a low self-esteem. Then one of her aunts took it upon herself to make Diana feel special. She complimented her, told her she never met a stranger, was kind and loving, and good in dramatic plays. For a child who felt of little value, the love of this one aunt has made a remarkable difference in her life. Diana says, "To this day, at age forty-three, I can't wait to talk to my aunt who lives about a thousand miles away. I know that again I will get to hear how special I am. Because of her faith in me, I have always tried to live up to her expectations."

Some of us—parents, aunts and uncles, grandparents, and teachers—don't realize the value of an encouraging word or the desperate need of a child to feel special in his troubled world.

After a church service where I'd spoken about silver boxes, a grandmother came up to tell me she had been saddled with the care of her three grandchildren, all under four years old. She hadn't realized that because of the resentment she has against her daughter, she had been taking it out on the children by saying hurtful things to them. Although they are not to blame for their unfortunate circumstances, they had been receiving the punishment. This lady told me that she had not realized the damage she was doing to these little ones by feeding them negatives about themselves and their mother. After hearing the Silver Box message, she said she was going to change her attitude and watch her words. Realizing the value of encouraging words in a child's life helped her to see what an awesome responsibility had been placed in her hands.

For each one of us, no matter where we are in life, there is a responsibility to make others feel special. We may be the only one to give that other person a much-needed silver box with a bow on top.

"An anxious heart weighs a man down, but a kind word cheers him up" (Proverbs 12:25, NIV).

11

A Box of Peace

*F*red and I were good Christian people, the typical American couple of the '50s. We had always lived exemplary lives as model citizens, as presidents of everything we touched, as regular church attenders. We had built the big house, driven the big cars, and achieved the big success. But after systematically doing everything right, I gave birth to two sons, one after another, both of whom were afflicted with a fatal brain disease. We could not believe that bad things could happen to good people. If there was a God, how could he let this double tragedy fall upon hard-working, positive-minded people like us?

Disillusioned and despondent, we gave up on church and put our image of God in a box on a shelf to be opened up at some future date if our boys were healed or our fortunes changed. We stopped going to church, for no one there appeared to care about our tragedy. They all seemed to be wrapped up in their own lives. Those who talked to us at all avoided any mention of our dying boys. Bad things weren't supposed to happen to good people in the '50s. These were the "Happy Days," and the mere sight of a mistake made people look in the opposite direction. Everyone was busy chasing rainbows, and the "'50s God" was a benefactor ready to shower prosperity, peace, and presents onto the success-seekers below. When for some reason we came up with a problem he didn't fix, we gave up on God, shoved him into a box, tied it up with rope, put it out of sight, and said, "From here on, I'll handle life on my own." *Time* magazine proclaimed "God is Dead," and we believed it.

Fred and I did the only thing we knew to do with grief: put the memories behind you, pretend it never happened, and get on with life. I went back into theater work and modeling, and Fred immersed himself in his restaurants all day and in his night club into the wee hours of the morning. Our denial of the deaths divided us emotionally, and our disappointment and depression distanced us from each other physically. We were mentally divorced from each other, and we set out to build separate lives in our own strength.

Spiritually we were both empty, and we each had a touch of guilt because we'd abandoned church and our perception of God. One day at a Christian Women's Club luncheon I heard a message that touched my hardened heart. The verses the speaker used were Romans 12:1, 2, "I beseech you therefore, brethren, by the mercies of God, that ye present your bodies a living sacrifice, holy, acceptable unto God, which is your reasonable service. And be not conformed to this world: but be ye transformed by the renewing of your mind, that ye may prove what is that good, and acceptable, and perfect, will of God."

For the first time, I caught the concept that my relationship with God was to be more personal than simply expecting him to give out big bonuses because I'd played the game of life so well. I was to present myself to the Lord, give myself away, become a silver box with a bow on top. And I was the only one who could present myself. It was a step of active faith. It was not my right to put God away and ignore him. Instead I should position myself before him as a living sacrifice, completely giving up my anxious plans and ambitions.

As the speaker explained, this act was reasonable and God would accept me as I was. I didn't have to say I was sorry, I didn't have to pledge I'd go to church, I didn't have to become a different person. I only had to give myself to God and let him transform me. I didn't even have to take a course.

The speaker asked if any of us had been conformed to worldly standards and had been disappointed in the results. I was surely a classic case of conformity. I had taken every all-American step to success and what had it gotten me: two dead sons and a dying marriage.

"But there is hope," the speaker said with loving assurance. "We can stop conforming to the world and allow God to transform our mind, renew our spirit." I knew I needed a new mind and spirit, and so I prayed with that man. And for the first time, I gave myself to the Lord; I became a gift, an offering to the Lord.

Some of you reading these words may be in difficult straits. You may be wondering how, when you had such high hopes for life, you got into the situation you're in today. Some of you have been reading this book seeking some personal word of encouragement, looking for the light, begging for a little silver box with a bow on top.

I know how you feel, for I've been there: looking, seeking, knocking. Jesus says he sees us there in despair, and he knocks at the door and when we are willing to open it, he will come in (Revelation 3:20). But we have to take the first step. We have to give ourselves up to him.

Picture yourself right now as an empty gift box. There's not much in there of redeemable value, just some crumpled tissue paper and an old wrinkled ribbon. Now wrap the box up in silver paper, put a bow on top and give yourself to the Lord Jesus. "Here I am Lord; reach out and take me. I'm wrapped up, decorated, shiny; I'm a living sacrifice, a gift."

Give yourself to Jesus today.

For he is the life, the truth, and the way.

God the Father knows what it's like to give sacrificially. He loved you and me so much that he gave his only begotten Son that if we would only believe in him he would give us everlasting life (John 3:16). When we give up, he doesn't leave us as unopened presents; he opens up new possibilities in our personalities and gives us a long-range benefit plan.

For each of us the gift of God is eternal life (Romans 6:23), and he promises that to all who believe on him and receive his gift, he gives the power to become his children (John 1:12) and adds the peace of God that passes all understanding (Philippians 4:7).

You and I have to take the first step of giving ourselves to the Lord. If you have never done this, pray with me now.

> Lord Jesus, I present myself to you today. I want to be a gift to you. I want to be a sweet-smelling aroma to the Father. I give up the control of my life to you and know you will receive me just as I am.

You've promised to give me peace, power, and eternal life if I'll but reach out and take your gift. I accept your blessing today and thank you for what you're going to do in my heart, mind, and soul from this day on and forever more. Amen.

Once you have presented yourself to the Lord and accepted his gifts to you, you will begin to know his perfect plan for your life. It may not be what you had in mind, it may not include wealth and worldly success, but it will give you peace of mind, the power to rise above your circumstances, and the pension plan of eternal life.

Karen writes:

My mother was sixteen years old and decided she wanted to marry my father, but the only way she could do that was to get pregnant. So here I came with a shotgun wedding. Mom was sixteen years old and Dad was twenty-three. He was hell on wheels—fast cars, fast women, and drinking. He did not want me and neither did my mom. She just wanted my dad. Two brothers followed between the fights, beatings, and moving here and there. Mom was always running away, Dad was messing around with other women, and I was told by my dad that it was all my fault that he was stuck with my mom. They eventually divorced.

Next my mom "played the field" until she met husband number 2, who had four children. I became the oldest of seven kids and had more responsibility. When I was in eighth grade my stepfather kept trying to get in my bed. One night, my mom caught him and sent me away to live with my dad and his girlfriend and their child. Dad was part of a motorcycle gang, and his girlfriend was a heroin addict. Dad set me up with some of his "friends" on dates. Then in tenth grade, when a friend and I went Christmas shopping, a police officer said that we were carrying drugs (which we were not) and we had to do what he and his partner wanted. It was horrible, and I don't know how we got home—home where no one cared what happened.

My life went on like this until I met Jesus. He forgave me and helped me to forgive my parents. But I could never forgive myself and believe I had some self-worth until I met you and Lana Bateman in 1987. You both helped me realize that I had a worth to God and that I needed to forgive myself and know that I had a purpose in this life.

I am now married and have two beautiful children and a teddy bear of a husband. I am active in my church, teaching Sunday school for the third- and fourth-grade girls. I feel I can't get enough or learn enough about the Lord and the Bible. It was you and Lana that helped release me from my bonds of the past, and it is you with your encouraging words and books that help keep me on the path of the Lord. When Satan tries his stuff, the Lord now has a hold on me and I know that I can rebuke Satan with the Lord's name, and I remember you and your stories of encouragement.

As Fred and I gave ourselves to the Lord, holding nothing back, he removed us from our home where the black cloud of death and dying moved quietly from room to room. He gave us a new beginning. At first the tiny cramped quarters he placed us in seemed like a step backward, but it was in Bungalow One, at the headquarters of Campus Crusade for Christ, that we first became a Christian family. It was there we began to study God's Word, to have a family prayer time, and to teach Bible studies in our little home. However, there's not enough room to move all of you into Bungalow One, and God has more originality than to run you all through the same process he used on us, but know he has a plan that is custom-tailored especially for you.

So wrap yourselves up in shiny paper and "present your bodies a living sacrifice, holy, acceptable unto God, which is your reasonable service" (Romans 12:1). He will transform your mind and give you a present in return, a box full of peace and power, tied up with ribbons of love, and tagged with the words "The gift of God is eternal life."

Receive this gift as a big silver box with a bow on top.

"Store up for yourselves treasures in heaven, where moth and rust do not destroy, and where thieves do not break in and steal. For where your treasure is, there your heart will be also" (Matthew 6:20–21, NIV).

12

Safe-Deposit Boxes

*T*he apostle Paul never took any charm courses or went to motivational business seminars. He never read *"How to Win Friends and Influence People* or saw videos on *The Seeds of Greatness.* He was physically unattractive, had a "thorn in the flesh," didn't drive an Italian car around Rome, and never had his hair styled. How could such an unsophisticated person maintain his popularity as an author for almost two thousand years? Because he knew the secret of giving out encouraging words to those who needed them. He carried a bag of silver boxes wherever he went. Even from jail, he sent out messages of joy and hope.

Paul and Silas left the prison and went to Lydia's house. There they met the believers, spoke words of encouragement to them, and left. (Acts 16:40, TEV)

After the uproar died down, Paul called together the believers and with words of encouragement said good-bye to them. (Acts 20:1, TEV)

When Paul taught the people about spiritual gifts, he encouraged them by telling them that everyone had at least one gift to be used for the edification of the body. While some are more obvious than others, "We are to use our different gifts in accordance with the grace that God has given us. If our gift is to speak God's message, we should do it according to the faith that we have; if it is to serve, we should serve; if it is to teach, we should teach; if it is to encourage others we should do so" (Romans 12:6–8, TEV).

Giving encouragement to others is a most welcome gift, for the results of it are lifted spirits, increased self-worth, and a hopeful future. Paul knew that whether a person was attractive, charming, and educated made little difference if the person was not used of the Lord to encourage others. When reviewing his own service to the people of Thessalonica he wrote, "You know that we treated each one of you just as a father treats his own children. We encouraged you, we comforted you, and we kept urging you to live the kind of life that pleases God" (1 Thessalonians 2:11–12, TEV).

Every letter Paul wrote, every message he gave included some word of encouragement.

It was in the fall of 1980 that the Lord used one of Paul's encouraging statements to Timothy to start me on a ministry of encouragement to others. In the previous ten years, I had gone from teaching Bible studies and giving my testimony at Christian Women's Clubs to speaking across the country and writing books. There had been no mentor showing me what steps to take, and I had learned the hard way, through experience.

Finally, all my years of work were bearing fruit, and I felt the Lord calling me to share what I'd learned with beginning speakers and potential writers. I had no time to write a course, and I wasn't sure if anyone would want to be trained. As I prayed for direction, I felt led to invite forty people to the seminar I had not yet written and see what the response would be. Within a short time I had thirty-five positive replies, and I was committed to forge ahead and write what became CLASS, Christian Leaders and Speakers Seminars.

At that same time, the Lord gave me a verse to confirm my calling to the ministry of encouragement. Paul wrote the verse, along with many others, to encourage young Timothy. Paul had sent Timothy off to Ephesus to oversee some fledgling churches, and he had not been received with open arms. The older pastors resented a young man coming in as a "district superintendent" and Timothy was ready to quit and come home. Paul gave Timothy a plan of how he could phase himself out of a job by preparing others to speak and teach in his place. As I studied this verse, I realized how well it applied to me at that time, and continually up to today, as I desire to share what I've learned with others.

Paul wrote to Timothy, "And the [instructions] which you have heard from me, along with many witnesses, transmit and entrust (as a deposit) to reliable and faithful men who will be competent and qualified to teach others also" (2 Timothy 2:2, AMP).

In applying this to myself, I realized I had been given many instructions basic to speaking and teaching. Starting with my father's encouraging me to memorize verses and poems when I was very young, I continued by taking elocution lessons in grammar school and winning the poetry reading contest in high school. I was in the senior class play and assisted the teaching director. In college, I became the student casting director for all the major musical comedies, the assistant to the Dean of Music, the winner of the New England Model Congress for presenting a political address, the top female debater, and the only one chosen to do honors work in speech.

I majored in English, speech, and education and became a teacher on both the high school and college levels. I'd been a professional president of numerous organizations and had become a Christian speaker and author. I'd worked hard to store up knowledge and experience, and I was ready to share the "instructions" which I'd read from Paul along with what I'd received from a host of teachers, pastors, coaches, directors, and encouragers along the way.

According to Paul, I should "transmit" the instructions which I had received—send them across from my mouth and mind to the ears of others; I should "entrust" it "as in a deposit." Obviously, we don't drop money into a trash can, nor should we throw instructions to the wind; they should be entrusted to those who can use the information in a positive way. They should be like a bank deposit, put into the bank where we have an account with the hope that if things go well we may someday get some interest on our deposit. We all want our treasures in "safe-deposit boxes," in the hands of faithful and reliable people. We wouldn't hand our money to just anyone who happened to be hanging around the bank and hope they'd put it into our account. We'd give it to the teller, a person we could trust, one who is faithful and reliable. So it should be with our instructions. They should be given to people who want to learn, who fit what we have to say, and who can be counted on to use the information wisely.

The purpose of taking the time and making the effort to transmit wise deposits into the minds of those who are eager to learn is so they will become competent and qualified to pass it on to others. For Timothy, the sooner he got others trained the sooner he could leave for home. For me, the more I train others to speak, teach, counsel, and write, the more I multiply the ministry the Lord has given me.

As I sat with a group of college students in a coffee shop after teaching an all-day seminar, one young man asked me, "How long have you been writing books?"

"Ten years," I replied.

He looked at me as one might stare at a sainted grandmother and said, "Why did you wait so long to get started?"

From his young perspective, it appeared that I had wasted my life until I was approaching senility, and it was truly a miracle that the Lord had redeemed my talent before I'd become too old to use it. I'd never looked at myself from his point of view, but in answering him, I recalled that when I was in college I had thought anyone over forty was ready for retirement.

Why had I waited this long to write? This young man's question caused me to reflect on my life and find the common thread that held the various events together. I told him that my whole life had been a preparation to get me ready to write: my childhood memorization, my high school plays, my college speech and drama training, my English and speech teaching, the loss of my sons, my Christian commitment, my Bible teaching, my speaking ministry. All these events had been leading me to put my life stories on paper and then to train others to do likewise.

I'm sure what I gave him was more of an answer than he

had expected, but his provocative question made me reflect on the broad span of my life.

Why did I wait so long to start writing? It took all that time to work through my traumas and tragedies, and to study, teach, and memorize God's Word. I needed time to test the results of my solutions for marriage problems, depression, and grief. It took time to realize that my hurts and victories could be used to give others hope. My whole life had been a training ground for Christian service. Our difficulties gave us compassion for the hurting and heartbroken. My love for teaching and experience in communication gave me the skills for a platform ministry. My background in English made writing a natural extension of my speaking. I'd had a fifty-year education of experience and preparation.

Oswald Chambers in *My Utmost for His Highest* wrote, "When God speaks, many of us are like men in a fog, we give no answer. . . . Be ready for the sudden surprise visits of God. A ready person never needs to get ready. Think of the time we waste trying to get ready when God has called!"

Once I understood that God could take any life submitted to him and use it to bless others, I wanted to help other people get ready. I wanted to show Christian women that God could make a ministry from their own lives and use them to comfort and instruct others in areas where they had experienced victory. Little did I realize in 1980 that this ministry would eventually bring me into a position of training pastors.

Based on 2 Timothy 2:2, my seminar program incorporates my lifetime of experiences and training and uses them to show others how to get ready for God's call. I am continually amazed to see how quickly God anoints a servant once he or she is prepared.

Marilyn Heavilin came to our program a year and a half after losing her teenage son to a drunk driver. Still going through the stages of grief, she didn't expect God to use her in any specific way. Once I heard how she had handled the loss of her son and the lawsuits that grew out of the accident, I asked her to share her story at a conference.

Shortly after that, on behalf of Mothers Against Drunk Driving (MADD) Marilyn began to speak to high school students about the potential tragedies of drinking and driving.

Next came invitations from The Compassionate Friends, a self-help support group for bereaved parents, to speak at their national conventions. In four years' time Marilyn's life has gone from that of a grieving mother with little direction to that of an author of four books and a guest on national TV and radio programs. At age fifty-one, she has begun a whole new life of purpose in comforting others because she was ready when the call came.

Seminar participant Georgia Venard, a registered nurse and a former drug abuser, became discouraged when her church told her not to mention her drug problems because they feared it would cast a bad light on them. Yet other church members had been quietly seeking her help. I encouraged her to put her solutions to substance abuse in writing and had her speak at a conference. Now in her forties, Georgia speaks frequently, counsels constantly, is on our staff, and will soon write a book on how Christians can overcome addictions.

Patsy Clairmont ran away from home at fifteen and didn't complete high school until she was forty. Because of her lack of education and feelings of insecurity, she couldn't imagine God could use her in a big way. When I first heard her give book reviews at a women's retreat, I was magnetized by her dynamic presentation and her electric personality. I invited her to our seminar and was impressed with her knowledge of Scripture, her hilarious sense of humor, and her testimony of overcoming agoraphobia—the fear of open spaces. She moves an audience from laughter to tears in a split second and she is now, in my opinion, the most dynamic woman speaker in the country. Patsy came to me with an open and teachable spirit, and now, in her forties, she is a seminar director and has a contract to write a book encouraging other women who feel insecure and lacking in training to get ready for that surprise call of God.

Bonnie Green (wife of John Green, composer and five-time Oscar winner) has been active in the Hollywood community for years. She invited me to speak for a few of her friends in her home. When I heard her life story, I asked her to come to a CLASS meeting with some of her friends. All were believing Christians, women in their middle years who had not felt comfortable speaking out for the Lord up to that point. Bonnie came to realize how many women were quietly suffering through the pangs of infidelity in their marriages, and she wanted to help them with the steps that had healed her emotional hurts. Bonnie now hosts a weekly prayer group and is writing her life story.

How about you? Have you felt you were too old (or too young) to be used of the Lord? Have you thought you didn't have the right education or background to speak, teach, counsel, or write? Has some discouraging person knocked the enthusiasm out of you? Have you failed to realize that your life experiences and God's Word provide the basis for a ministry?

Stop now and evaluate your life. Has there been a common thread of interest or talent that you have overlooked?

Do you realize that God can work with any available vessel who's willing to be filled with his power and spirit? Do you realize that God's Word says you are to comfort others with the same kind of comfort God has given you? Don't wait any longer. Ask God today where he would like you to go and what he would like you to do. What a shame it would be if he called and you said, "Wait awhile, Lord; I'm not ready yet."

The days are short, the times are perilous, the people are hurting. Get ready for the call of God.

Why did I wait so long to get started? I guess it took a long time to get me ready, but now that God is using me to train others, I want to encourage you to get moving. My silver box for you is to open your eyes to your own possibilities. God can make something beautiful out of your life.

I continue to be amazed at how God works through CLASS. When it was started, the intent was to train women to be speakers. While that is still the main thrust, God has "expanded our coast" so much further. For many, like Delores who attended CLASS in Florida, it is the start of a new direction for their life. Delores wrote to me, "I truly do thank God, and I thank you for the way you have touched my life! I could listen to you forever! Your mind and color-filled words fascinate and intrigue me. I will never again be content with average! I have been going through a restless time in my life, and I feel you have helped to give me the tools to begin digging through some things. I feel equipped to start being all that I can be. Thank you for your big silver box with a bow on top to me!"

I thank Delores for sending me this silver box, interest on my deposit.

Silver boxes come in many forms. Whatever the form, they are often thought of as a prized possession. When we developed the curriculum for the Advanced CLASS, I never thought that the video in the little black box we send home with each participant could turn into a silver box. Each person comes to Advanced CLASS with two brief prepared presentations which are videotaped. After participants complete their messages, I give an evaluation, and my comments are added to the tape that they take home.

Annie Rodriguez attended the Advanced CLASS in the summer of 1988. After hearing me speak on Silver Boxes, she sent me this note. "The videotape from Advanced CLASS is one of my most prized possessions. Not because of what I performed on it, but because of your gracious, complimentary, and encouraging words about what I had presented. These are the Silver Boxes you have given to me."

When I hear that someone who has come to CLASS is passing on to others what he or she has learned, I consider this interest on my deposit. Occasionally the interest is not only intrinsic, but financial as well.

Dear Florence,

Enclosed is a check for fifty dollars. Please accept that as a gift for giving to me much needed confidence. I know it says in the Scripture that a teacher is to be paid for their giving.

I have already used many of the points that you taught, especially the "Silver Box" visual. I spoke on self-esteem to a group of 150 third-graders. They received their Silver Box. Many thanks for sharing that idea (plus many more) where these ideas of hope will change the lives of many in a greatly needed positive way.

Charmed, confident, and committed,
Mary Anne

From the beginning of CLASS, Fred has been extremely supportive. In the last several years, he has divested himself of any other businesses to travel with me and handle all schedules, book sales, and facility arrangements. Because he has a compassionate heart, he has been able and willing to counsel those who have emotional hurts or spiritual confusions. From listening to the multitudes of problems, Fred began to examine his own childhood and found rejection and suppressed anger. He submitted himself to some counseling and uncovered the causes of his repressed emotions. In August 1987, Fred began a process of restoration which included the daily writing of his prayers to the Lord. Usually he writes for a full hour a day and many times for two or more hours.

As his close walk with the Lord brought healing, people came to him with their hidden pains of the past, and he was able to help them uncover the cause and lead them into a route of recovery and onto a road to restoration. We became a new team: I spoke and caused people to examine themselves, and Fred counseled those who had memory gaps or confusions about their identity. Amazing results came from his selfless care and concern for hurting Christians, and at the age of fifty-nine, Fred found that God had a whole new plan for his life that neither of us had contrived in our minds.

"The steps of a good man are ordered by the Lord" (Psalm 37:23).

Fred took the instructions that he had gained from prayer, Bible study, counseling, reading, and CLASS and began to transmit them to those in need so that they could put their lives back together and ultimately become competent and qualified to pass on the benefits of their healing to others.

In May 1988, Fred gave a workshop on the adult effects of childhood trauma at a women's retreat. The response from this kept him counseling in the prayer room until 2:00 in the morning and every half-hour all the next day while I was speaking. As we flew home from this retreat of 800 women, we looked at each other and Fred said, "We have got to put something in writing to place into the hands of these hurting women. We can't leave them with open wounds bleeding. We've got to give them something tangible to add help to their hope."

I agreed and suggested doing a few typed pages that would offer some specific steps toward restoration. Fred felt we needed to write a book with our combined knowledge and experience. Since I was at that time in the midst of writing both *Raising the Curtain on Raising Children* and *Personalities in Power,* I could not even entertain the idea of another book. With my heavy travel schedule I couldn't see my way clear to finish what I had already started. Fred assured me if the idea was valid, the Lord would somehow make the time for us to write it.

Fred had never written a book or even an article. He had disliked high school essay writing although he got good grades on the grammar and punctuation. The teachers told him that he wrote well and if he ever had anything to say, he could probably do quite well. Fred finally had something to say.

Because of the pressure I already had on me to meet deadlines for the two books I had in progress, I made a deal with Fred. If he wrote the outline for the new book, assigned which one of us would write each topic, and then wrote all of his part, I would then write mine. I figured I had allowed for several contingencies. If he failed anywhere along the way, I wouldn't have to write anything. If the Lord's hand was on this book, Fred would become an author; if not, I hadn't spent my time on it.

Within a few days Fred handed me a complete chapter outline. He then organized his material and went away for two weeks to write. When I saw the pile of pages he returned with, I knew the Lord had directed our path, and I must heed the call and get to work. I wrote my part without reading Fred's, and he pieced the two manuscripts together. I researched appropriate verses for the headings, and Fred proofread the final copy. To this day I can hardly believe we sent a manuscript off to the publishers that I had never read from beginning to end.

The editor of the book changed very little and sent the manuscript to a Christian psychologist to read for content approval. The psychologist not only applauded the material but added a handwritten note saying, "Although there are two names as coauthors, it is obvious that only one person wrote this."

What a testimony to the creative power of our Lord that when he inspires and directs, there is unity of purpose and harmony of construction. The two authors became one. Instead of my writing and Fred's writing patched together, we had His writing making the whole greater than the sum of its parts. Of all the books I've written there's never been one so inspired, created, and blessed of the Lord as *Freeing Your Mind from Memories that Bind.* There has never been such excited response. There have never been so many testimonies of healing. None of my fifteen books has sold so many so fast as this one.

During this whole process, Fred's life has changed. He's emptied out the burdens of his past and his well of suppressed anger. He's gone from being my backstage defender, arranger, and encourager to having a whole new ministry as a compassionate comforter to a multitude of hurting people. He's now an author in his own right. He is in demand for talk shows on radio and TV on a subject that is just emerging as a topic of discussion in the Christian community.

Most exciting to me is the transformation that the Lord has skillfully brought about in Fred's life in less than two years, because Fred was willing to examine his life deeply, bring his needs to the Lord, study God's Word, write out his prayers daily, saturate himself in helpful material on the subject, and then be willing to be used in ministering to others.

One interviewer who has known us for years asked, "What's happened to you, Fred? You have a new vitality and energy that I've never seen before."

Because Fred's been faithful and reliable to the calling of the Lord in his life, God has rewarded him with a gift of insight and perception which enables him to help people get to the source of their problems in a matter of hours. As he counsels, he calls on the power of the Holy Spirit to reveal truth to the person in need so that they may bring the pains of the past before the Lord for his healing touch. No longer are these hurting Christians putting Band-Aids over their symptoms, but they are finding the source of their dysfunction and accepting the Lord's solution.

I never set out to train my husband, but he has become my prize pupil, and I am so proud of what he's allowed the Lord to do in his life. I have put my words into a large savings account, and it is already returning interest on my investment. I am so grateful for the ministry of encouragement that the Lord has given me, for the desire to take what I have learned in sixty years of life and pass it on. I am grateful that he enables me to transmit it to others, to hold back no secrets but to entrust what I have experienced into the hearts of faithful and reliable people like Patsy, Bonnie, Georgia, Marilyn, and Fred, as well as my children and countless others, who in turn teach and bless others in need and give them hope.

I won't live on this earth forever, but I will leave behind a trail of silver boxes, and the Lord will continue to tie big bows on the top of each one.

"'For I know the plans I have for you,' declares the Lord, 'plans to prosper you and not to harm you, plans to give you hope and a future'" (Jeremiah 29:11, NIV).

13

Receiving Silver Boxes

A little word in kindness spoken,
  A motion or a tear,
Has often healed the heart that's broken,
  And made a friend sincere.

Then deem it not an idle thing
  A pleasant word to speak;
The face you wear—the thoughts you bring—
  The heart may heal or break.

From "A Little Word"
By Daniel Clement Colesworthy

Frequently people ask, "What if you want to give out silver boxes, but people won't receive them?" There are several reasons that people may be uncomfortable with compliments:

1. The compliment doesn't fit their individual personality pattern.
2. They've been told since childhood that they're homely, dumb, or dirty.
3. They were abused as children.
4. They are going through a difficult time at the moment.
5. They've been told that to accept praise is unspiritual.

Let's start with the lightest of these reasons for why people won't accept our joyful words of congratulation. *Understanding a person's personality pattern can help you to know what kind of compliments he or she will welcome.* People are not all the same, so many of us make mistakes when we try to give others the kind of compliments we want to hear. Then we get hurt when they don't receive our words with enthusiasm.

Many of you who have read my books *Personality Plus*, *Your Personality Tree*, and *Raising the Curtain on Raising Children*, are well aware of the four basic personalities and have no doubt been using them as guidelines for *Getting Along with Difficult People*. For those of you who have not become familiar with this simple tool, let me give you a quick review.

The Sanguine is the *popular person* who wants to have fun out of every situation and be the life of the party. Sanguines love to talk.

The Choleric is the *powerful person* who wants to take control of every situation and make decisions for others. Cholerics love to work.

The Melancholy is the *perfect person* who wants everything in order and done properly and who appreciates art and music. Melancholies love to analyze.

The Phlegmatic is the *peaceful person* who wants to stay out of trouble, keep life on an even keel, and get along with everybody. Phlegmatics like to rest.

It is amazing how quickly we can learn to spot these people and therefore know how to approach them correctly.

The Sanguines are the easiest to spot because they make grand entrances, love attention, attract people with their magnetism, exude charisma, and tell funny stories. What they want to hear from you is how attractive they are, how you like their hair, make-up, dangling rhinestone earrings, or anything else they have put on to ensure that you notice them. They live for the externals and want you to get excited over their clothes, sense of humor, or new red sports car. If you are a Melancholy, you will not naturally be given to praising the obvious and will feel that to laugh at the Sanguine's jokes and stories will only encourage that person to babble on.

No matter what your personality is, if you wish to give a silver box to a Sanguine, make sure it is large, shiny, and covered with sequins—and present it in front of a large, adoring audience.

The Choleric Powerful Person is easy to spot because he walks with authority and appears to be in charge of everything. Such people don't want to waste much time on trivial activity with no obvious results or converse with people who have nothing to say of any consequence. They are frequently telling other people what to do and pointing out the "dummies" of life. They accomplish more than any of the other personality types, can quickly assess what needs to be done, and are usually right. They don't need to be affirmed on their looks, but they love praise for their accomplishments; their speed in problem solving; their constant goal setting; their loyalty to God, church, mother, business, or country; and their sense of fair play. If you are Phlegmatic you get worn out just watching these people, but if you want them to be impressed with you, tell them how amazed you are at how much they accomplish in a very short time. They may never have noticed you before, but they will suddenly see you as a person of great discernment.

The Melancholy Perfect Person is usually very neatly put together and intellectual looking. These people are usually quiet, reserved, and a little ill-at-ease in social situations where they don't know everyone. They would rather talk quietly to one person in depth than banter with a group. They consider compliments on clothes and external niceties to be trivial and want to hear about the inner virtues of integrity, wisdom, and spiritual values. They often marry Sanguines who can't find their way inside to these deep virtues and who keep telling them how cute they look. When we don't understand these differences, we are giving out silver boxes that nobody wants. The Melancholy is very sensitive and easily hurt and tends to take what others say in humor as personal and hurtful. Since Sanguines and Cholerics say whatever comes to their minds without weighing their words, they often deflate the Melancholy who is waiting for someone to hand him a silver box that says, "I understand you."

The Phlegmatic Peaceful Person is amiable, easy to get along with, and relaxed. These people fit into any situation, blend in with the wallpaper, and modify their personality to get along without conflict. They laugh with those who laugh and cry with those who cry. Everyone loves the low-key nature of the inoffensive Phlegmatic, and though they aren't loud like the Sanguine, they do have a witty sense of humor. They often lean while standing and sit in comfortable recliner chairs if at all possible. They don't need a lot of praise like the Sanguine, nor do they want to be in charge like the Choleric, or get too deeply involved like the Melancholy. They do appreciate being noticed once in a while, being included in conversations that they won't push into on their own, and being told they are of value and their opinion is respected. Since they often marry Cholerics, whose idea of value is wrapped up in how much is accomplished in a given day, they don't get appreciated for their quiet and gentle spirit. They, in turn, find it difficult to praise the constant projects of the Choleric because it wears them out just thinking of them.

Even with this brief section on the personalities, I hope you will see that each type appreciates a different size and shape for their silver box.

One of the reasons some people cannot receive compliments is that they have been programmed from childhood to feel totally unworthy. Many of us heard negative comments from our parents that may have damaged our sense of self-worth, and we have a twinge of doubt as to whether or not we deserve a compliment. The people who were physically, sexually, or verbally abused as children know there is no good thing about them. There is no doubt or questioning in their mind. As Fred and I counsel individuals who may look attractive and put together on the outside, but who have the inner symptoms of abuse or rejection—we find that underneath they think they are ugly, stupid, and immoral. Many people who overspend on their clothes and constantly have their hair restyled, or at the other extreme, those who dress sloppily and let their hair hang over their faces, are attempting to either overcome or validate the feeling that they are ugly. When you compliment their clothing, they can't believe your words are sincere.

Juliene grew up with emotional abuse and as a small child felt "alone, dirty, and like scum." She had been put down so much she had a very low self-esteem. When her youth pastor told her she had on a pretty dress and had a pretty face, she couldn't believe him. Her mind wanted to accept his compliments, but her emotions wouldn't allow her to feel worthy of them. He continued patiently to build her up and eventually made her feel she was "somebody" and respected.

"He made me believe I was a person acceptable to God and others, that I was a lovable, likable person and that God really did care about me and maybe other people would care about me, too."

Without the kind and affirming attention of the youth pastor over a period of years, Juliene might not yet be able to accept a silver box of any size.

Some who keep taking classes and getting degrees are in a hopeless quest to overcome their feelings of stupidity caused by some kind of abuse. When I talk with a person who is fanatically pursuing education, I ask, "Who told you you were stupid as a child?" Often they burst into tears at the question, and they usually know who it was. Frequently, the demeaning parent abused them physically or sexually as well as verbally. When you tell these people how smart, clever, or witty they are, they can't believe you.

In the other extreme, a child who is made to feel stupid gives up on any kind of education and doesn't even try.

Jane was her "daddy's girl," but when she was eight, he disappeared to spend the next twenty years in prison. She missed him so much that she wrote him a letter each day. In the third letter he wrote her, he told her she had the worst handwriting he'd ever seen. That little innocent child was so crushed at her daddy's comment that she never wrote him another word. For the next nineteen-and-a-half years she never heard from him. Jane said he died without either one of them breaking the painful silence.

Can you imagine if you, a stranger, were to comment positively on Jane's handwriting what a chain of memories it would trigger? She might react so strongly that you would be offended, but if you knew what was inside her, you'd understand.

Jane concluded, "I've never been able to give other people silver boxes. Thank you for giving me my next step. It's time to write and grow."

Dottie wrote me that her parents always said, "The boys got all the brains." And she believed them!

"I never felt I could rise to the level of my brothers' abilities. I wasn't a good reader, and I was a bit overweight and larger than the other girls my age. The teachers expected more of me, and they put me down when I couldn't read well out loud in front of the class. They confirmed my inability, and I accepted defeat."

As so often happens, we marry a person who does the same negative things our parents did, and Dottie married a deeply melancholy man who had a superintellect, a critical spirit and who put down her lack of education. He reinforced her belief that she lacked intelligence, and they later divorced after her feelings of self-worth had hit bottom.

Faced with a life alone, she asked the Lord where to turn. She got a job in sales, where she was amazed at how well she could do. Dottie is now back in college getting A's and B's.

"I never thought I could do it." She says in amazement.

People who were sexually abused as children, whether or not they remember the incidents, have basic feelings of guilt, blame, filthiness, and immorality—even though they were the victims. Because their body was violated, they mistrust people and expect the worst to happen—and it often does.

Often when we try to compliment the victims of sexual abuse, they will reject our good words. Their emotional computers throw out our compliments because they don't "compute" with what they have been programmed to believe.

For a person who is not in tune with the "victim personality," this may not make sense, but I often can tell how a person was victimized by complimenting them in the areas of looks and figure, brains and competence, standards and spirituality. If the person instantly rejects one of these, it gives me a clue to what type of abuse he or she was subjected to as a child.

Even if these are new thoughts to you and you have no interest in dealing with other people's victimization, at least let this information give you a subconscious reference point as to why certain people cannot handle your positive and affirming remarks. If you are someone who wants to understand the pains of your own past or the residual effects on others, please read our *Freeing Your Mind from Memories That Bind.*

Since the publication of that book, we have been deluged with mail from Christians whose adult lives are a wreck because of childhood abuse or extreme deprivation and rejection.

Bertha wrote a letter that sums up how the abused person feels when compliments are extended.

> I remember when I was thirteen and my mother called me a slut and a whore. The words were spoken shortly after a season in my life when I had been molested by one of her boyfriends. I still continue to feel like a harlot, dirty, and unlovely.
>
> Now I'm recently married, and I cannot receive my husband's love, and I shrink away from his touch. I came to this retreat praying the Father would meet with me. He has in some ways, but I know it will take some time to discard the effects of childhood abuses. I have found that at times it is difficult and almost impossible to receive silver boxes from others when all the input in my life has been mostly negative and destructive.
>
> Maybe in your book you could give words of wisdom to those of us who are not able to receive these gifts. There are times when we do not believe or trust in the intentions of those gifts. May the Lord continue to bless you as you are a gracious instrument used to encourage many of us who have hurts such as these.

When you read her words, you can't help but feel extreme pity for a girl who was sexually abused by her mother's boyfriend and then put down and called names by the mother who laid the blame on the victim. No wonder she feels worthless. No wonder she has sexual dysfunction in marriage. No wonder she can't accept silver boxes.

Stefanie grew up thinking she was worthless. Her mother died young, her father was an alcoholic, and her aunt raised her begrudgingly. The aunt told her she was her slave and made her do demeaning things, such as pulling up her nylons and attaching them to the garters on her girdle. Having grown up with a slave mentality, Stefanie couldn't believe she amounted to anything. All her life, she had suppressed her anger, but she knew she had some emotional problems when she snapped at her two year old child, "I'm not your slave!"

After two years of counseling, she was able to realize that her aunt, who was now dead, was still controlling her emotions. She learned that she was taking out on her little child the anger that she couldn't ever give to her demanding aunt.

When we realize that many of the people we talk to each day have had some kind of abusive background, we can accept negative reactions without taking them personally, and we can reach out with compassion instead of withdrawing in a huff.

Likewise, in reserve situations, when we wonder why a certain person can't seem to give anyone a silver box, we might consider the possibility that this person has never received one. It's hard to give what we've never received. When one has been made to think he's of little worth, when his opinion of himself is low, he doesn't think anything he might offer to another in the way of words or gifts would be of value. He is so afraid of being laughed at, of demeaning himself, that he holds back from giving blessings to others.

Sometimes when people are ill, have just heard bad news, have some momentary chemical or sugar imbalance, or are depressed over current circumstances, their response to compliments will not be normal. If you call a friend with cheery thoughts, a friend who usually responds well, and that day she cuts you off or won't accept your good humor, don't take it personally and become depressed yourself. You somehow hit that person at a wrong moment. It wasn't your fault and probably not hers either. Just back off for now and try again later.

Aletha wrote me a letter with a perfect example of this problem when she tried to give a silver box to a friend just out of surgery:

> I really appreciated your lesson on Silver Boxes with Bows on Top. I have never been made so aware of words and their effect on people before. While we have always tried to watch our words to others, the idea of having our blocks knocked down was never stressed, neither was the idea of how to handle this when it happened. Tonight I'm writing you as I'm unable to sleep yet at 1:30 A.M. The reason? I went out today and purchased flowers to take to a friend who had surgery on Monday. I called her this evening at 8:30 to see if I might come to the hospital tomorrow and bring them to her. Her answer is the reason I'm not sleeping. "No," was what she said. "The idea was sweet of you, but you can just find some other nice lady to take them to."
>
> We are not teenagers, Florence. She and I are both over fifty and have been friends for several years. Why I'm feeling let down, I haven't quite figured out, but my silver box with a bow on top seems to be a bit crushed and unraveled. Tomorrow I think I shall find someone who would like to receive red roses and so make a new box using the pieces of the old. There can never be too many silver boxes with a bow on top.

I wrote Aletha and asked for permission to quote her letter. When she sent approval, she added a follow-up to the previous letter:

I did receive a lovely thank-you note from my friend for the flowers I didn't give her. I did take the flowers and spread my silver boxes to three other people. This was an enjoyable experience, but the first glow had been removed. My fault I'm sure!

It's really nobody's fault. Aletha did a kind and generous act by buying flowers for her friend who was perhaps drugged after surgery or so surrounded by flowers that she felt she was laid out at her own funeral. In either case, she didn't want the gift at that moment, although she did write a gracious note of thanks for Aletha's thoughtfulness. Three other people were blessed, and we have been able to use this as a teaching example to help us not get upset or feel rejected if someone doesn't want what we have to give.

Another reason some people can't accept compliments is that they were trained from childhood that good Christians must be humble to the point of feeling no self-worth at all. I remember asking my mother why she never gave me compliments like Peggy's mother did, and she said, "You never know when you'll have to eat your words." When you are told that to be spiritual you must adopt Paul's "in me is no good thing" theory or that if you get compliments it will go to your head and you'll become cocky, you grow up feeling guilty if someone hands you a silver box. Underneath you don't feel you deserve it because of the "humility brain washing," and on the surface you think you can't accept compliments and remain spiritual.

Melissa's father was a pastor, and she was raised in a superspiritual home. In high school, her parents told her she was vain and kept her from fitting in with the other girls. She was never allowed to dress like the others or shave her legs. She always felt she was on the outside looking in. As she grew up, she was socially insecure. Recently she dared explain to her parents, now in their sixties, how her feeling of being left out in her teen years and their peculiar brand of religious self-denial has warped her whole personality for life. She fully expected her saintly parents to say they were sorry, or at least admit that in retrospect, they were too strict. Instead the father looked at her coldly and said, "We discussed it at the time and decided it was good for your character that you learn to live with hatred."

Melissa was devastated by this heartless remark, and when she talked with me a few weeks later, she shook when repeating it. It is only by the grace of God—not her parents—that Melissa has any sense of self-value or, for that matter, is even a Christian today.

When someone like Melissa receives a compliment, he or she subconsciously rejects it immediately. Only with prayerful retraining can this person feel worthy of a silver box, even a little one.

In reading this section, if you have said to yourself, *I just can't accept compliments,* you might ask yourself why. Is it because others have not understood your personality and have unwittingly said things that hit you the wrong way? Things that you felt were insincere? If that sounds possible to you, spend some time in a study of the personalities so that you can meet the needs of others and accept their compliments graciously, realizing that they will speak out of their natures without necessarily understanding yours. When you begin to sense the strengths and weaknesses of other people who are not like you, you will be able to overlook their poor choice of words and to be grateful for any kindnesses.

Beyond acceptance will come a sensitivity to recognize that the type of compliment the other person gives you is what they are craving for themselves. If a Sanguine raves about your dress that you don't even like, know she is hoping you'll like hers. If a Choleric is impressed with all you've accomplished, when you feel "it's all in a day's work," know he'd like you to ask how much he's done today. If a Melancholy sees something deep and meaningful in what you've said, don't say it was an accident; just thank her for being so analytical and perceptive. If a Phlegmatic thanks you for sitting with her at a social event and you've said nothing of consequence, don't point that out, but instead tell her what an easy and pleasant person she is to be with and that you hope you can sit with her again the next time.

Without realizing it, so many people hurt the person who is holding out the silver box because they simply don't know how to accept it with a thankful heart.

If you've been told all your life that you aren't too bright or beautiful and you refute all praise with "I'm really not very smart," or "This is actually an old (cheap, ugly) dress," or "I just hate my hair today," you insult the judgment of the giver and show how insecure you are at the same time. Perhaps it is time you reappraise yourself and prayerfully rid yourself of these inaccurate preconceptions so that you can accept positive words with appreciation. Remember, when we turn gifts down often enough, people stop giving them to us. The lady who refused the roses didn't get them offered again the next day, for they were already given to three other people who were receptive. Be grateful for any offer of kindness, and thank the giver for his or her thoughtfulness. Silver boxes are too precious too refuse.

If you realize that you can't believe any good thing about yourself and you tend to be suspicious of those who seem too cheerful, perhaps you have some residual effects of childhood rejection that you have never dealt with. Perhaps you have not been aware that growing up in some type of dysfunctional home could still be affecting your self-worth today. If you are easily hurt or depressed or feel people who praise you are insincere or hypocritical, you may need to look back and dig out the root of your insecurities.

If you find that at certain times of the month you are irritable, that when you have a headache you get nasty, that when work has gone poorly you take it out on the family, realize that this erratic behavior is difficult for others to understand. Sometimes we hope if we ignore our pain, no one else will notice it. But it is better to express how we are feeling and ask others to understand than to bottle up our emotions and then let our anger fly on the first person who triggers it. My children could always tell when I was stretched to my limit, and they'd say, "Mom, I think you need a rest. Go lie down and I'll finish the dishes."

If someone tries to be kind at a time when you can't accept it and you snap at them, immediately let them know you're sorry. It's not their fault. They were doing their best. It's just been a very bad day. People can accept a minimal explanation far better than a feeling of rejection.

If you have been led to believe, by your parents or your church, that to accept any affirmation is unspiritual, that self-depreciation is next to godliness, that any feeling of frivolity is sinful, and that you are to pick up your cross daily and drag it through life, perhaps this is the time for you to step on the worm of unworthiness. Religious people often portray a grim picture of piety, but a look in God's Word shows the value of encouragement and the virtue of a joyful heart. Don't let a legalistic religious background hamper your happiness and your ability to accept a compliment. When you throw down a silver box that has been offered, the donor doesn't see this rejection as a matter of spirituality, but as a personal affront.

Some of us feel that as good Christians, we should serve sacrificially but not allow other people to do anything for us. While this giving attitude seems spiritual, it is more often an insecure need to be sure we have the upper hand and that the scale will always tip in our favor. Let those who wish to give you blessings bestow them upon you, and then thank them graciously. The Lord allowed Martha to serve him and the woman to pour expensive perfume upon his feet that they might feel rewarded. The Lord inhabits the praises of his people, and we should be willing, thankful, and honored to receive silver boxes with a grateful heart.

"The words of the Lord are flawless, like silver refined in a furnace of clay, purified seven times" (Psalm 12:6, NIV).

14

Boxes of Broken Dreams

As I began to speak on silver boxes and to see the reaction it brought from the audience, I had to look back in my own life and see where the encouragement had started for me. Who gave me silver boxes? I could quickly recall some hurtful comments: "It's a shame she didn't get curly hair like her brothers. . . . Why is it the boys always seem to get the looks? . . . Aren't they adorable!" (And then about me) "She must be smart." I thought again of that lady who said to my mother about us three, "It's a shame there's no hope for those children, as they appear so bright." Hardly a silver box!

I grew up knowing I'd better be smart, as I was not going to make it on my looks—if I were to make it at all! I studied hard in grammar school to get all A's and became almost a compulsive student in high school, knowing that if I couldn't get a scholarship to college, it was all over for me. There would be "no hope." I'd end up in the shoe factories where all the other poor kids in Haverhill landed.

The threat of continued poverty, routine and boring work, and a dull, drab existence motivated me to learn everything I could. Francis Bacon wrote in 1597, "Knowledge is power." Samuel Johnson said in 1759, "Knowledge is more than equivalent to force." I believed them both and determined to store up an abundance of knowledge, that someday I might have power to control my circumstances.

My father saw in me a quick, open mind and began to pour knowledge into my head from the time I sat on his knee. He taught me the Christmas story from Luke when I was three and encouraged me to recite it in the church pageant. Before I went to kindergarten, he taught me to respond to a difficult question by saying, "Not knowing to any degree of accuracy I dare not assert for fear of erring therein."

He had a whole series of Little Willie poems he taught

the three of us. And even though I found them easy to learn I didn't always understand the meaning. For example:

> Little Willie had a mirror
> He lapped the back all off
> Thinking in his childish error
> 'Twas good for whooping cough.
> At the morning of the funeral,
> Mrs. Jones said to Mrs. Brown,
> "'Twas chilly for little Willie
> When the mercury went down."

Although I recited this as a little child, I was a teenager before I realized that mirrors were backed with mercury. Suddenly Little Willie's death made sense.

Father taught me that "brevity is the soul of wit," as Shakespeare says in *Hamlet*. And he gave me an example I still remember, about the newspaper reporter who was too wordy. His editor told him to cut the news to the core and use as few words as possible. His next article was:

> Little Willie,
> Pair of skates,
> Hole in the ice,
> Golden Gates!

While these little items may sound like sheer nonsense, they represent time that my father spent with us, teaching us things that were fun. He encouraged us to broaden our vocabulary and to enunciate clearly. "If you can speak well, use your words correctly, and talk faster than everybody else, you will always get jobs over people that mumble." Little did our father realize as he emphasized the value of the spoken word that all three of us would grow up to be speakers.

Not only did Father encourage us to be the best we could, but he gave a ray of hope in the dark days of the Depression to the customers who came in discouraged over life's disappointments. When people had no money for a loaf of bread, he'd give them one. When they needed a listening ear, he'd sit down and talk with them. When the barber in the attic over our store came home drunk, my father would get up in the night and drag him up the stairs to bed. When my mother complained about working seven days a week in the store, washing all our clothes by hand in the slate sink, or trying to find another way to cook Spam—all legitimate complaints—my father would cheer her up and say, "It could be a lot worse. We all have our health."

We used to sing the old favorite:

> Home, home on the range,
> Where the deer and the antelope play,
> Where seldom is heard a discouraging word,
> And the skies are not cloudy all day.

My father would facetiously question what the "home on the range" must look like with all those deer and antelope romping through the living room. We'd laugh at the thought of it and then come back to the point of the song. It doesn't really matter where you live—on the range with all those animals, or in three rooms behind a store—if you give each other encouraging words, the skies are not cloudy all day.

The following story about my dad appears in my book *Your Personality Tree*, but I tell it again here because it illustrates so well "boxes of broken dreams."

When I was a senior in college, I came home for Christmas vacation and anticipated a fun-filled fortnight with my two brothers. We were so excited to be together we volunteered to watch the store so that my mother and father could take their first day off in years. The day before my parents went to Boston, my father took me quietly aside to the little den behind the store. The room was so small that it held only a piano and a hide-a-bed couch. In fact, when you pulled the bed out, it filled the room, and you could sit on the foot of it and play the piano. Father reached behind the old upright and pulled out a cigar box. He opened it and showed me a little pile of newspaper articles. I had read so many Nancy Drew detective stories that I was excited and wide-eyed over the hidden box of clippings.

"What are they?" I asked

Father replied seriously, "These are articles I've written and some letters to the editor that have been published."

As I began to read, I saw at the bottom of each neatly clipped article the name Walter Chapman, Esq.

"Why didn't you tell me you could write?"

Here I was a senior in college studying creative writing and I had no idea my father had produced articles good enough for publication.

"Why didn't you tell me you'd done this?" I asked again.

"Because I didn't want your mother to know. She's always told me that since I didn't have much education I shouldn't try to write. I wanted to run for some political office also, but she told me I shouldn't try. I guess she was afraid she'd be embarrassed if I lost. I just wanted to try for the fun of it. I figured I could write without her knowing it, and so I did. When each item would be printed, I'd cut it out and hide it in this box. I knew someday I'd show the box to someone, and it's you."

As I looked through the box I found a letter on the bottom from Henry Cabot Lodge, Sr., our Senator from Massachusetts. I couldn't imagine what Lodge was doing writing to my father. I'd never seen actual Senate stationery before and I asked, "Why did Lodge write to you?"

My father replied, "I sent him a letter suggesting how he could increase the efficiency and effectiveness of his next campaign, and this is his letter back explaining which suggestions he could and could not use."

I read the letter over and found it was not a form letter but a point-by-point reply to what my father had written. It began:

> I have your most kind letter of May 11, 1923, and am very grateful to you for your remembrance and for your pleasant words of friendship and congratulations which I assure you I both value and appreciate.

I was impressed! A senator had written to my father. I looked at my father in a new way that day. Suddenly he became a writer instead of a father with a limited education.

I put the letter back in the bottom of the box and placed

the clippings on top. As I looked up at my father, impressed with his accomplishments, I noticed his big blue eyes were moist. "I guess I tried for something too big this last time," he said.

"Did you write something else?"

"Yes, I sent an article in to our denominational magazine to give some suggestions on how the national nominating committee could be selected in a more equitable manner. It's been three months since I sent it in, and they haven't published it yet. I guess I tried for something too big this time."

This was such a new side to my fun-loving father that I didn't quite know what to say, so I tried, "Maybe it'll still come."

"Maybe, but don't hold your breath." Father gave me a little smile and a wink and then closed the cigar box and tucked it into the space behind the piano.

The next morning our parents left on the bus to the Haverhill Depot where they took a train to Boston. Jim, Ron, and I ran the store, and I thought about the box. I'd never known my father liked to write. I didn't tell my brothers; it was a secret between Father and me. The Mystery of the Hidden Box.

Early that evening I looked out the store window and saw my mother get off the bus—alone. She crossed the Square and walked briskly through the store.

"Where's Dad?" we asked together.

"Your father's dead," she said without a tear.

In disbelief, we followed her to the kitchen where she told us they had been walking through the Park Street Subway Station in the midst of crowds of people when Father had fallen to the floor. A nurse bent over him, looked up at Mother, and said simply, "He's dead."

Mother had stood by him stunned, not knowing what to do as people tripped over him in their rush in the subway. A priest said, "I'll call the police," and disappeared. Mother straddled Dad's body for about an hour. Finally an ambulance came and took them both to the city morgue where Mother had to go through Dad's pockets and remove his watch. She'd come back on the train alone and then home on the local bus. Mother told us the shocking tale without shedding a tear. Not showing emotion had always been a matter of discipline and pride for her. We didn't cry either, and we took turns waiting on the customers.

One steady patron asked, "Where's the old man tonight?"

"He's dead," I replied.

"Oh, too bad," he said and left.

I'd not thought of him as "the old man," and I was hurt at the question, but he was seventy-three and Mother was only fifty-three. He'd always been healthy and happy, and he'd cared for frail mother without complaint, but now he was gone. No more whistling, no more singing hymns while stocking shelves; *the Old Man* was gone.

On the morning of the funeral, I sat at the table in the store opening sympathy cards and pasting them in a scrapbook when I noticed the church magazine in the pile. Normally I would never have opened what I viewed as a dull religious publication, but just maybe that secret article might be there—and it was.

FOR MORE DEMOCRACY

A real ballot, such as the one I have suggested, would create interest and would ensure a cordial greeting for new delegates who are a little hesitant about coming forward. The new delegate would be sought out where now he feels neglected. Sad to say, the average member does not have enough interest or perhaps it is initiative to protest in the meetings, or even in this humble way. The ordinary member is apt to believe, as has been true so much in the past, that everything to do with church elections is cut and dried; therefore, he stays away and many times the church loses a valuable worker.

I took the magazine to the little den, shut the door, and burst into tears. I'd been brave, but seeing Dad's bold recommendations to the national convention in print was more than I could bear. I read it and cried, and then I read it again. I tucked the magazine behind the piano with the box, and I didn't tell anyone about it. My father's box of broken dreams remained a secret until we closed the store two years later and moved in with Grandma, leaving the piano behind. I gave my last look to the empty kitchen with the old black stove standing staunchly alone, while the bottle of kerosene gurgled loudly in the corner. I went quietly to the den, and as if in some religious rite, I reached behind the old piano where I'd practiced lessons and played hymns on Sunday evenings and pulled out the box—the box of broken dreams.

How grateful I am that my father showed me that box on that special day, or I never would have known the talent that he had. It has been passed down to my brothers and me and to our children.

Father left me no money, but he left me the box. He had little education and no degrees, but he gave me and my brothers a love for the English language, a thirst for politics, and an ability to write. Who knows what Father could have done with just a little encouragement? Had he been given a few silver boxes here and there, would that have made a difference?

I'll never know what Walter Chapman, Esquire, could have been. Was there a great American novel inside him, or at least a weekly column for the *Haverhill Gazette*? Could his charm and sense of humor have brought him political acclaim?—or could he at least have been the mayor of Haverhill?

I kept that cigar box full of clippings and the magazine with Dad's article in it hidden away for thirty years. When I wrote my first book, *The Pursuit of Happiness,* I remembered the box, and I pulled it out. I framed the article next to a picture of my father and his church membership card that had also been in the box. When I went back to Boston from California to refresh my memories, I went to a store that featured old pictures and autographs of famous people. They had one photo of Henry Cabot Lodge, Sr., which he'd signed at the bottom. I bought it and had it framed along with his letter to my father. I have these two framed memories on the wall in our study, and each time I look at them I realize the value of an encouraging word.

How many of us have lived with a parent or mate whose true talents we've never known? How many of us have discouraged others in their pursuit of a career that didn't seem logical to us?

I remember the high school English teacher who listened to my desires to be an actress. She didn't tell me that my dream was ridiculous, although I know she must have sensed I'd never make it to the big time. Instead, she encouraged me to take all the speech and drama courses the college had to offer so I'd be prepared. Then she added, "But always have a Plan B." She combined positive words on a career in the arts with the realistic caution that I'd better have a plausible occupation to support me while I waited to be discovered.

Few of us will ever make our livings as writers, actors, musicians, poets, artists, or dramatists, but we should never wipe out the possibility. We should encourage ourselves and others to pursue our dreams, "But always have a Plan B" to fall back on.

Oliver Wendell Holmes once said, "Many of us die with the music still in us."

Why is it that so few of us ever fulfill our potential? Is it because somewhere along the line someone whose opinion we valued gave us discouraging words?

As a child, Francis Steckman dreamed of being an artist. She loved spending all her spare time painting and drawing. But at the age of fourteen Francis heard some discouraging words. Her mother said, "You will starve if you expect to earn a living through your art work."

Francis told me, "I gave it up right then and there, and never felt I had any talent. About eight years ago my husband encouraged me to try again. Now I paint as a hobby, and it makes me feel really good. I regret the years I wasted because of those discouraging words."

After listening to me tell the story of my father, Deanne Davis used this example to open up some much needed communication with her husband. She wrote:

> We have been married almost twenty-one years, have a good marriage, and love each other, but recently it hasn't been enough for me to live in his shadow any longer and just do what he is doing when I have so much I want to do myself. I feel that I have gifts and talents, too, and would so much like to use these. Needless to say, this has caused some friction . . . some distance . . . maybe some resentment, and certainly a lack of understanding.
>
> Recently we went out to dinner together, and on the way home I related the experience you had with your father. My husband was very touched, for he has always felt that no matter how closely you live with your children, they have no idea in the world who you are, and your story certainly validated that feeling. I went on and spoke of the silver boxes and told him that that is what I want to do more than anything, to give silver boxes in my world, to give hope, to try to make people laugh and see Jesus and the joy of life all at the same time.
>
> I, of course, began to cry before I could get through it all as these thoughts had so touched my heart. He, too, was moved to tears and, I think, has a better idea of what is the matter with me. I have been trying to get him to understand that I've raised the children, I've done all that stuff, and now I want to enlarge my horizons and do new things.

As Deanne's husband understood for the first time her sincere desire to speak and help others with encouraging words, he no longer felt threatened by her desire to communicate truth to those in need.

When I first met Woody at our CLASS, I was impressed with his handsome looks and his obvious confidence in himself. As a successful businessman, he appeared to have life under control, but as we talked, he said he wished he could write.

"Why can't you?" I asked.

"When I was in high school and had to write essays, my teacher told me I had no talent and shouldn't try to write. I believed her and I've never written since—not even a letter."

"How have you handled your business without writing?" I asked.

He responded, "I hire people to do all my writing for me."

I encouraged him and told him that since he was such a good speaker, I was sure he could write if he could just put that teacher's remarks behind him.

With my affirming words, Woody changed his opinion of his abilities, and since that time, he has written several books and has started his own publishing company, where he helps to start writers who have ideas that have a very limited audience. He often speaks at writers' conferences to encourage others, and he also has started a newsletter for Christian writers and speakers. An encouraging word had never been heard, but for Woody one encouraging word was all it took.

While Judy did not have a dream for her own life, she was fortunate enough to have someone else who did. It wasn't her own mother or father, but her friend Michelle's mom who encouraged her. During her high-school years, Judy decided to become a Candy Striper with her friends. She had no real desire to do volunteer work in the hospital, but when all the other girls were doing it, being a "junior nurse" seemed like a great idea. She bought her red and white striped uniform and prepared to serve the sick. During this training time, she had a disagreement with some of the other girls and decided this volunteer stuff wasn't for her anyway.

Judy says, "So I called up my friend Michelle to offer her my uniform which I had already bought. Well, Michelle wasn't home, but her mom answered the phone and offered to take a message. When I told her about the uniform, this wise woman said to me, 'Why are you letting the other girls' opinions influence you? You are smart and kind. There are lots of people you could really help. Of all the girls, I feel you would be the best for the job. I know you are smart enough to not pass this up because of unkind friends.'"

This positive comment made Judy stop and think in a less emotional way. As it turned out, Judy was the only one who stuck with it. She decided to make nursing a career, and at this point, she has been a nurse for sixteen years! Judy makes her job an opportunity to witness to others. She told me, "God uses me during early morning hours to minister to patients who are recovering from surgery. All due to Michelle's mom's words of encouragement, I have a job that brings me joy. I don't know where I would have been now without her. During multiple times of unemployment for my husband, this job has been our survival."

My daughter Marita wrote to me about her friend Sherry. "It is hard for me to imagine a person having a strong interest in an area and being told things like 'you'll never make it,' 'you're not smart enough for that,' and 'Why in the world do you want to do that?' I see now that I was blessed to have come from an encouraging environment. I have talked to so many who heard discouraging words, that I now realize the kind of home I grew up in was an exception to the rule.

"My friend Sherry had always wanted to be a doctor. When she expressed interest in that direction, her mother told her she'd never make it. Sherry told me, 'So I never tried.' Sherry grew up feeling that she was not worth anything.

"Recently Sherry gave her future to the Lord, and he opened up a new direction for her to enter. She graduates with a bachelor's degree from San Diego State in May, and she will enter a student teaching program in the fall. Sherry won't be a doctor, but she is excited over the prospects of being an encourager to young people in need."

Andrew Murray states: "From the beginning, the young Christian must understand that he has received grace with the definite aim of becoming a blessing to others. Please do not keep for yourself what the Lord gives to you for others. Offer yourself expressly and completely to the Lord—to be used by Him for others. That is the way to be blessed over-flowingly yourself."[5]

When we, like Sherry, offer our futures to the Lord, we can expect "to be blessed overflowingly."

We all need encouragement. We can live without it just as a young tree can live without fertilizer, but unless we receive that warm nurturing, we never reach our full potential, and like the tree left to itself, we seldom bear fruit. My father did not produce much fruit in his lifetime: a few clippings and a letter from a senator. He never lived to see even one of his children become a success in life, but because of his feeding our minds and our spirits, because of his fertilizing our creativity, we have all become healthy trees bearing much fruit.

As the most popular radio personality in the city, my brother Ron encourages the people of Dallas, Texas, each morning with his verbal handholding. Advertisers pay top dollar for thirty seconds on his show because they know he can deliver results. Because his listeners believe in him, they have kept his show number one for over twelve years. According to the *Dallas Morning News*, [6] which published a full-page picture of him along with a three page article, Ron's "audience loyalty is legendary." They told of his now-famous promotion in April 1988 when as an off-the-cuff filler he asked his listeners to send him twenty dollars—for no special reason. Within three days, he received over $240,000 with no strings attached. He gave it all to local charities, including the Salvation Army. The article pointed out that "audience trust was at the heart of Chapman's most successful promotion." They quote him as saying, "The fact that we can make you feel good about yourself and make you laugh when you don't want to, is an enormous service. My show is patter, but it's much deeper than that, I'm convinced, or I wouldn't be doing it."

Giving out encouraging words, keeping Dallas happy, and doing it all with humor and style has brought Ron the 1988 *Billboard* Award as "Air Personality of the Year," the outstanding radio personality in adult contemporary music in the United States.

About our father, Ron says, "He worked the store like a stage. You could never get him out of there because that was his love. I've got a show; he had a store."

We all grew up in that store, which was our training ground for living with and encouraging people. It was our stage, our rehearsal for a creative life. My brother Jim inherited my father's gift with words, along with my mother's musical ability. He has written both the words and music to many songs, he has conducted musicals, and he writes many of his sermons in verse. As a career chaplain in the Air Force, he received the Outstanding Young Chaplain Award for the entire Strategic Air Command. With two bachelor's degrees and two master's degrees, he has used his talents to minister to others in preaching, teaching, and counseling. He is currently the pastor of the Bath Church in Bath, Ohio. He has raised six outstanding children who are all creative and who are the enduring fruit on his family tree.

In his 1988 Christmas message to his congregation, Jim shared, in verse, the Christian commitment we need as parents to prepare our children for today's world.

> Whenever a parent teaches a child the wonderful
> Gospel news,
> Whenever a parent makes a commitment, and Christ is
> the one she will choose,
> Whenever a parent makes Christian decisions in the
> face of many temptations,
> That parent prepares in the heart of that child Jesus
> Christ's incarnation.
> Whenever a businessman stands for what's right and
> defies all the idols of gold,
> Whenever he does what his conscience commands him,
> the message of Jesus is told.
> Whenever a doctor works long in the night to heal a
> pain-ridden soul,
> Whenever she gives of herself to restore him, she acts
> in our Christ's healing role.
> Whenever a teenager stares down temptation and
> follows the tough, narrow way,

Whenever he chooses the morals of God, he has
  brought that much closer Christ's day.
Whenever a lawyer cares more for what's right than for
  what he might possibly gain,
Whenever he risks his credentials for justice, our Lord
  is repaid for His pain.
Whenever a teacher brooks the frustration of insolent
  kids and their folks
To reach for the one child who is longing to know, she
  removes the mind's crippling yokes.
Whenever each one of us knows of another who needs
  to know that we care:
How we love one another, rejoice in His Word, are
  really a people who share
And reach out to that brother, lift up that sister in
  Jesus Christ's sacred name,
We wash from their souls, remove from their minds the
  hurt and the guilt and the shame.
Whenever we, as the Church of our Master, respond
  (for our blessings are many)
To those who around us, without our compassion,
  would hardly be found with any.
Whenever we do this, as one or a body, in the Name of
  the Babe in the manger,
We help clear the way on the highway of God for the
  hurt and the poor and the stranger.

Although my father died with the music still in him,
leaving us no money, but only a box of broken dreams, his
legacy of love, of creativity, and of encouraging words will
carry on in the three of us and our children and their children. We are the products of the silver boxes he wrapped up
for us. We won't die with the music still in us.

"Hope deferred makes the heart sick; but when dreams
come true at last, there is life and joy" (Proverbs 13:12, TLB).

15

Music Boxes

*I*n all the years Fred and I have been married, I never felt I knew his mother. She was always outgoing, warm, and friendly, but somehow I never knew what she was really like inside. I admired her ability to entertain graciously, to dress tastefully, and to converse engagingly. She was one of those people whom we all know, impressive but somehow untouchable, someone who has built an invisible wall around herself. And while you can't see the partition, you can feel the barrier between you.

Mother always kept activity swirling around her. I realize now that this constant busyness was to keep her mind from having time to look at herself realistically or from letting others peer inside. We had a congenial but artificial relationship until one rare evening in her Miami condominium when we found ourselves together with no party going on at all.

I wondered what to say to her. We'd never really talked before. All that came to me was that old cliché, "What was it like when you were young?"

She responded happily and began to tell me of her experiences going through Cornell University. Suddenly she looked younger and more radiant than I'd ever seen her before. "I had this boyfriend," she said excitedly. Somehow I'd never thought of my mother-in-law as having a boyfriend. "He was so handsome and so much fun. He was going to be a lawyer, and I was so in love with him."

"What happened?" I asked, sensing that this story didn't have a happy ending.

"Well, I brought him home one weekend, and my mother asked him about his family. Later my mother told me he was not for me as his family didn't have enough money. My mother always said, 'You can fall in love with a rich man as easily as a poor one.' We continued to see each other, and by the time we graduated, we were engaged to be engaged. We were each going in different directions for the summer, but in the fall he was going to call me, and we'd get together."

"What happened then?"

Suddenly she stopped, her face tightened, and she said simply, "He never called."

"He never called?" I asked.

"He never called."

"Why didn't you call him?"

"Girls didn't call boys in those days; plus very few of us had phones. I just waited, and he never called."

The story had come to a jolting end. As I groped for an appropriate comment, she added, "But that's not the end of the story. I went to a party a few years ago, and as I looked across the room, I saw a man in his seventies who had the profile of that young man I'd loved. I moved where I could look up in his face, and as I did, he glanced down at me and said in surprise, 'You're Marita.' I answered, 'You're John.' As we stood in a state of pleasant shock, I asked that one question that had been in my mind all those years, 'Why did you never call?' 'Oh, I called all right,' he said, 'and every time I called, your mother answered. She told me each time that you didn't love me, that you'd asked her to tell me not to call again, and the last time I called she said you were engaged to another man!'"

As Mother told me this unbelievable story, she sobbed out, "My mother's words ruined my life."

After we cried together, she finished the story. Her mother had introduced her to Fred Littauer, saying he was "a nice man from a wealthy family. They're in the silk business."

She dated him on the rebound, and they were married. As she concluded her story, she added, "But I never was in love with him. Oh, I learned to care about him, and I had his five children. He was a good man, but I never was in love with him."

To break the silence that followed I asked, "What would you have been if you could have been anything you wanted to be?"

"An opera singer," she answered quickly. "I wanted to study music, but my parents felt that was a waste of time, that

I'd make more money in the millinery business. But I was in one show in college, and I had the lead."

She got up quickly, went to a closet, and pulled out a box of old pictures. She showed me a large photo of a stage setting with the cast posed for review. "There I am." She pointed proudly to a confident and beautiful young girl seated on an ornate chair, center stage, the obvious star of the show.

I'd not known of her operatic ambitions before, and I shared with her how I loved the theatre, and had wanted to be an actress until my drama teacher told me I was much better at directing others.

We looked at the picture of her on the stage and then she handed it to me. "Here, you can have this. Give it to your daughter Marita. She's named after me. Let her know that her grandmother could have been an opera singer if only she'd been encouraged."

I had that picture copied so that Marita has one and so do I. Often I show it when I speak on silver boxes, and I am constantly amazed at how many people come up to tell me about their musical talent that was stopped in its tracks by a discouraging word. Of all the comments and letters I have received, the subject of music is the most prevalent.

When Tammi was in the fourth grade, she tried out for the class singing group. Somehow, during the selection process, the teacher told Tammi that she could not sing and shouldn't try out again. Because of this, she never sang again. And when her son wanted to audition for the church youth choir, she discouraged him, saying he had "such a little voice" that he wouldn't be chosen.

Isn't it amazing how we tend to do to others what was done to us without even making a connection? When she was thirty, Tammi confessed to her mother that she had never sung because of the teacher's comment. "I was so shy, it embarrassed me that I failed." Yet when her son was ready to step into a similar situation, her negative emotional response was to keep him from trying out to spare him possible rejection.

All these years have passed, and Tammi still can't pick up a hymnbook in church without hearing the teacher say, "You can't sing."

How careful we should be with our words, when we consider the lasting power for good or evil of one hastily spoken sentence.

James 3:6 says, "The tongue is like a fire. It is a world of wrong, occupying its place in our bodies and spreading evil through our whole being. It sets on fire the entire course of our existence with the fire that comes to it from hell itself" (TEV).

We must not let the fire of unkind words sweep through our bodies and out our mouths.

After hearing me speak on silver boxes, Pat told me this story about her daughter who is now fifteen. "When she was three or four years old she loved to sing. She always sang, but she was especially vocal in church. Often our pastor would go out of his way to tell her how much he enjoyed her song, and the choir invited her to join them when she was older. She was so proud! Now, please understand, her words were not the words in the hymnal, nor were most of her songs the ones the rest of us were singing, but I always knew that her songs were a joyous sound in the Creator's ear.

"One day my mother came with us to church. She didn't understand the fragile heart of a child, didn't know what her words would do, and to this day wouldn't understand. When the music began, and we all stood to sing, my daughter began to loudly proclaim her praises, 'Jesus Christ, happy birthday, I love you.' My mother told her to be quiet, she was too loud, she didn't know the words, and she was embarrassing. My daughter never sang again. In fact, to this very day she rarely sings, and she never sings very loud.

"Your silver box message reminded me of this incident

and the insensitivity I experienced from my mother during my own childhood, but also I felt such sorrow for my mother. I suppose she never knew much kindness either. Oh, but such joy I've experienced knowing that I have tried so hard to give my children kind words and now those words have a name, silver boxes! The best presents in life are silver boxes because they last the longest!"

The silver box message has inspired many to turn around and give a silver box to the person who gave them so many. Mr. Aldstadt was an encouragement to Kim when she was in junior high school. After hearing me speak, she decided to send him a tape of the silver box message with a note of thanks for his encouragement to her. Kim said, "Mr. Aldstadt was my spring of fresh water when I was drowning in an ocean of negativity." Kim grew up in a home where little positive was ever said. During the time she was in Mr. Aldstadt's class, her two grandmothers died, her grandfather was molesting her, both her parents were alcoholics, and she had to be the parent to her siblings. Kim was surely living in an "ocean of negativity."

Kim played the viola and Mr. Aldstadt was her music teacher. While she was not a fantastic musician, he always encouraged her and told her she was talented. He asked her to help teach the new students and told her she was the only true alto teenager he had ever heard. He made her feel welcome at school and smiled at her in the halls. She auditioned for the All-City Junior High Orchestra, and although she had been placed in the last chair, he allowed her to sit in the first chair. Ten years later, when Mr. Aldstadt was teaching Kim's little sister, Kim visited the class. Mr. Aldstadt had her stand up, and he told all the students how talented Kim was. He truly was a spring of fresh water!

Mr. Boettgu had a unique way of encouraging his students that Sally Cummins has never forgotten. Mr. "B," as they called him, was her high-school music teacher. Each week he would choose one person from the class and write his or her name on the blackboard. Then everyone had to think of something good and positive about that person. He went around the room and each person shared a good comment, and he would add that idea to the growing collection on the blackboard. Sally wrote, "When my turn came, I copied the list and carried it around with me wherever I went. When I felt bad, I would get it out, carefully unfold it, and read the treasured comments. It always made me feel so much better."

Michelle played the clarinet in her fifth-grade band class. She really wanted to play the flute, but her sister's clarinet was "going to waste" and her parents couldn't afford to buy another instrument. She didn't enjoy the clarinet, but since she loved music and the clarinet was all she had, she gave it her best. The sounds it made were discouraging, and she wasn't allowed to practice as much as she wanted to because of chores and homework. Michelle told me, "I felt I'd never get better." Even in class the clarinet squawked and made awful noises that were so bad they made her cry in frustration. Mr. Pelossi, the music teacher, kept encouraging her anyway. When she would cry, he would hug her and say, "Just keep practicing; you'll be the best." Throughout high school, he was Michelle's mentor, friend, and substitute dad. She says, "I'll never forget him. Praise God for planting him in my life!"

After hearing the silver box message a year ago, Gayle wrote and told me this story. "In my home there weren't many words spoken, either encouraging or discouraging. But I did have a teacher in eighth grade who was an encourager for me. She suggested that I try out for a girls' choral group. I was accepted, and that was the start of my love for singing that is just beginning to creep back to the surface. It was an eight-member Christian folk group, and I toured with them throughout Southern California for two years. During that time, no one from my family ever came to hear me nor did they express any interest in what I was doing. Though they never gave me discouraging words, the lack of silver boxes devastated me so much that I never sang again."

Now a full year after a seed was planted in Gayle through the silver box message, she is beginning to "hear the music again." Gayle, don't die with the music still in you.

As a young girl, Sandy dreamed of joining a singing group in her mother's family who were very musical and were often invited to sing at different churches. She spent hours learning all the words to the songs and developing her part so that when she was old enough she could join them. She practiced by herself when no one was home. One night she was cleaning up the kitchen and was singing one of the hymns at the top of her lungs. Unbeknownst to her, her mother and her aunt had come in and heard her singing. She went into the dining room to wipe the table and overheard a conversation between her mother and her aunt.

"Did you hear Sandy singing?"

"Wasn't it pitiful?"

As Sandy sadly related this story to me, she said, "To this day I have never sung in front of anyone but my grandchildren. Recently while I was singing to my grandson, Evan, he put his tiny hands up to my cheeks and pulled my face a little closer and said, 'Granny, you sing so pretty!'"

All these years Sandy has put aside her love for singing. While she might never have been a great performer, Sandy could have had the joy of singing if she had just had a little encouragement.

Sing for joy to God our strength;
  shout loud to the God of Jacob!
Begin the music, strike the tambourine,
  play the melodious harp and lyre.

Psalm 81:1–2, NIV

A pastor told me he had always wanted to play the violin. He took lessons as a boy and practiced a lot. He was proud of how well he was doing, and his teacher encouraged him. But one day he heard his father yell to his mother, "Will you shut that boy up; I can't stand that screeching any longer." The boy shut up all right. He told me, "I put the violin down, and I've never picked it up again!"

At the age of fourteen, Kristina Lemons loved to play the piano. She dabbled with different variations of the songs she played and wrote an entirely new song. She was playing on the piano one day in the church basement when the pastor's wife came in and listened. She encouraged Kristina and asked her to play the song for "special music" in church.

Kristina remembers a special silver box she got that day: "After I played the song in church, a lady came up to tell me that it was the most beautiful song she had ever heard. She asked me who wrote it. When I told her I wrote the song, she was amazed and promised to pray that I could write more beautiful music like that song. She said it should be published. I never felt more inspired to write music in my life."

We all know that making a living in art, theater, or music is not easy. In Judy's family, her interest in being a dancer was not only discouraged, it was ridiculed. Her parents made fun of her and told her that she could never be a dancer because she was just too big. Judy recalls, "In fact, in my family if you did anything that was clumsy, it was called 'pulling a Judy.'" This constant reminder of how klutzy she was caused Judy to give up any thoughts of dancing, and she went through life expecting to trip and drop things.

Many years later, she got a surprise letter from her mother. In the letter, her mother explained that she had never been able to tell Judy that she loved her or that she was pretty, but that her mother did want her to know that she loved her and she was proud of her. What a shame that Judy's mother's words came so late in their relationship. In another circumstance, Judy's father also wrote her a letter telling her that he loved her. Judy said, "I don't think he'd ever told me that before. These letters are all I have left of my parents now. I treasure these two silver boxes."

While speaking on the campus of a Christian university, I gave the silver box message to the students. Dinah came up afterward to tell me that she related to Fred's mother as she had wanted to be a singer from the time she was a child. "I grew up as a black in the deep South, and we were told from the beginning that there was no hope for us. I sang for fun, but I didn't ever expect to do anything with music. I studied hard and got into this school. Then I took a music class, and the teacher told me I had an unusual voice and I should try out for a part in the opera *La Bohême*. I'd never even seen an opera, but I went to the tryouts and got the part of Mimi. I can't believe that a poor black girl could ever have a leading role in an opera."

How grateful Dinah was for the teacher who gave her the much-needed encouraging words.

One Sunday morning after I had given the silver box message at a church service, a young man with sad eyes approached me. "Do you have any idea what doors of our minds you have swung open today?" I looked in wonderment as tears came to his eyes and he choked out, "You made me see what I could have been if only someone had encouraged me."

"What could you have been?" I asked.

"I could have been a pianist, but my family hated to hear me practice, and they nicknamed me Liberace. Each time I'd go to play they'd say, 'Get out the candelabra; he's going to entertain us again.' I couldn't stand the teasing so I quit."

"How old are you?"

"I'm twenty-six."

"You're still young. You can start again," I said positively.

"But they don't think I'm any good."

I then explained to this discouraged young man that he had two choices. He could go through life emotionally crippled by the words of his family. Or he could realize that they probably thought they were being funny and that he should put their demeaning words behind him and get on with his music.

"But every time I sit down to play, I hear them laughing at me."

This sensitive, melancholy young man named Jim had been so negatively conditioned by his family's words that he couldn't imagine putting the hurts behind him and moving on.

I tried a different approach, "Do you realize that when you refuse to continue your musical pursuits, you are allowing your family to control your life? Even though they are not present in your living room, they are in control when their past remarks dictate your present behavior. They have probably forgotten about their comments, yet you are allowing their former opinions to keep you from functioning fully today."

Suddenly his heavy eyes brightened up. "They have been controlling me, haven't they?"

"Yes, they have," I answered. "Don't you think it's time you grew up and threw off the restraints of the past? You're twenty-six. Should your parents still be in control of your emotions?"

"I guess I never thought of it this way."

"Who should be in control of your life?" I asked.

"The Lord Jesus?" he answered with uncertainty.

"That's right," I responded.

"Romans 12:1, 2 tells us that we are to give up the control of ourselves to the Lord, that we are to allow him to transform and renew our minds so that we will know what is the good, acceptable, and perfect will of God for us. Do you think God's will is for you to be held down and discouraged, for you to live a frustrated life because you never fulfilled your potential or used the talent he gave you for his glory?"

At this point Jim was in tears, and he put his head down on my shoulder and sobbed. I began to pray that God would lift the negative thoughts from his mind that were crippling his progress in life. I asked God to free him from the chains of the past that had him in emotional bondage. By the time I said "amen," he was breathing normally, and he looked up with a slight smile.

I suggested he start practicing immediately and mention to his mother he was going to begin playing again to check her current reaction.

Two weeks later I received a letter from Jim telling me he had never felt so good in his whole life. He had called his mother and dropped the thought that he might like to play the piano again. He was dumbfounded when she said, "It's about time. We've all wondered why you quit because you used to be so good at it."

"Imagine," he wrote, "I've spent all these years controlled by words that I guess they didn't mean. But finally I'm free to be me."

In Mother Littauer's last years her brilliant mind faded, her memory left her, and her ability to articulate ceased. When we went to visit her, we found her beautiful but silent. She smiled at us as if we were some pleasant passing strangers who had stopped by for tea. When we tried to talk to her, she looked at us as if we were speaking a foreign language. To see this woman whom we remembered as dynamic and powerful sitting silently and staring beyond us gave us an eerie feeling, as if we were supping in a sepulcher with the living dead. She could eat and move mechanically, but her mind and her mouth had been disconnected.

I asked the nurse who cared for her, "Does Mother ever talk?"

She replied, "Oh no, she never says a word."

As we discussed the tragedy of a once brilliant mind gone dead, the nurse made an interesting comment, "It's the strangest thing. She can't talk, but every so often she sings opera."

The nurse, who knew nothing of mother's repressed desires, marveled at how she could stand and sing when she couldn't say a word.

Isn't it amazing that those unfulfilled dreams are stamped so indelibly in our minds that even when all else is lost, those memories are not erased?

The night before Mother died, the nurse later told us, she stood by her chair after dinner and began to sing. She put on a moving performance and the nurse clapped in approval as Mother bowed and smiled. The next morning when the nurse went in, Mother was lying with her hands folded across her chest and with a smile on her face. She had sung her last song on earth and had been applauded by the angels.

Mother had talent that was never developed, a music box that was never allowed to play, a career that was never begun.

Mother died with the music still in her.

Over the last few years, as I have shared the story of my father's box of clippings and Fred's mother's box of old pictures—both boxes of broken dreams, boxes full of what might have been—people have flooded me with stories of their repressed desires, desires that were dismissed and dismantled by a careless word, a sarcastic comment, or a fear of failure. I've talked to so many who have had high hopes that were dashed against the rocks of reality by a parent who meant to be practical but killed a dream in the process, to so many whose emotions died with the music still in them.

Do you know someone who has—

A song waiting to be sung?
Some art waiting to be hung?
A piece waiting to be played?
A scene waiting to be staged?
A tale waiting to be told?
A book waiting to be sold?
A rhyme waiting to be read?
A speech waiting to be said?

If you do, don't let them die with the music still in them.

I will sing of the love of the Lord
    forever;
with my mouth I will make your
    faithfulness known through all
    generations.

—Psalm 89:1, NIV

Notes

1. David Dunn, *Try Giving Yourself Away,* (New York: Prentice-Hall, Inc., 1947), 4.

2. Ibid.

3. Ibid.

4. Florence Littauer, *Raising the Curtain on Raising Children,* (Waco, TX: Word Books, 1988), 299.

5. Andrew Murray, *Living the New Life,* (Springdale, PA: Whitaker House, 1982), 137.

6. *Dallas Morning News,* February 5, 1989.

Personality Profile

STRENGTHS

1	Adventurous	Adaptable	Animated	Analytical
2	Persistent	Playful	Persuasive	Peaceful
3	Submissive	Self-sacrificing	Sociable	Strong-willed
4	Considerate	Controlled	Competitive	Convincing
5	Refreshing	Respectful	Reserved	Resourceful
6	Satisfied	Sensitive	Self-reliant	Spirited
7	Planner	Patient	Positive	Promoter
8	Sure	Spontaneous	Scheduled	Shy
9	Orderly	Obliging	Outspoken	Optimistic
10	Friendly	Faithful	Funny	Forceful
11	Daring	Delightful	Diplomatic	Detailed
12	Cheerful	Consistent	Cultured	Confident
13	Idealistic	Independent	Inoffensive	Inspiring
14	Demonstrative	Decisive	Dry humor	Deep
15	Mediator	Musical	Mover	Mixes easily
16	Thoughtful	Tenacious	Talker	Tolerant
17	Listener	Loyal	Leader	Lively
18	Contented	Chief	Chartmaker	Cute
19	Perfectionist	Pleasant	Productive	Popular
20	Bouncy	Bold	Behaved	Balanced

Personality Profile

WEAKNESSES

#				
21	Blank	Bashful	Brassy	Bossy
22	Undisciplined	Unsympathetic	Unenthusiastic	Unforgiving
23	Reticent	Resentful	Resistant	Repetitious
24	Fussy	Fearful	Forgetful	Frank
25	Impatient	Insecure	Indecisive	Interrupts
26	Unpopular	Uninvolved	Unpredictable	Unaffectionate
27	Headstrong	Haphazard	Hard to please	Hesitant
28	Plain	Pessimistic	Proud	Permissive
29	Angered easily	Aimless	Argumentative	Alienated
30	Naive	Negative attitude	Nervy	Nonchalant
31	Worrier	Withdrawn	Workaholic	Wants credit
32	Too sensitive	Tactless	Timid	Talkative
33	Doubtful	Disorganized	Domineering	Depressed
34	Inconsistent	Introvert	Intolerant	Indifferent
35	Messy	Moody	Mumbles	Manipulative
36	Slow	Stubborn	Show-off	Skeptical
37	Loner	Lord over	Lazy	Loud
38	Sluggish	Suspicious	Short-tempered	Scatterbrained
39	Revengeful	Restless	Reluctant	Rash
40	Compromising	Critical	Crafty	Changeable

NOW TRANSFER ALL YOUR X's TO THE CORRESPONDING WORDS ON THE PERSONALITY SCORING SHEET AND ADD UP YOUR TOTALS.

Personality Scoring Sheet

	SANGUINE POPULAR	CHOLERIC POWERFUL	MELANCHOLY PERFECT	PHLEGMATIC PEACEFUL
1	Animated	Adventurous	Analytical	Adaptable
2	Playful	Persuasive	Persistent	Peaceful
3	Sociable	Strong-willed	Self-sacrificing	Submissive
4	Convincing	Competitive	Considerate	Controlled
5	Refreshing	Resourceful	Respectful	Reserved
6	Spirited	Self-reliant	Sensitive	Satisfied
7	Promoter	Positive	Planner	Patient
8	Spontaneous	Sure	Scheduled	Shy
9	Optimistic	Outspoken	Orderly	Obliging
10	Funny	Forceful	Faithful	Friendly
11	Delightful	Daring	Detailed	Diplomatic
12	Cheerful	Confident	Cultured	Consistent
13	Inspiring	Independent	Idealistic	Inoffensive
14	Demonstrative	Decisive	Deep	Dry humor
15	Mixes easily	Mover	Musical	Mediator
16	Talker	Tenacious	Thoughtful	Tolerant
17	Lively	Leader	Loyal	Listener
18	Cute	Chief	Chartmaker	Contented
19	Popular	Productive	Perfectionist	Pleasant
20	Bouncy	Bold	Behaved	Balanced
TOTALS				

Personality Scoring Sheet

WEAKNESSES

	SANGUINE POPULAR	CHOLERIC POWERFUL	MELANCHOLY PERFECT	PHLEGMATIC PEACEFUL
21	Brassy	Bossy	Bashful	Blank
22	Undisciplined	Unsympathetic	Unforgiving	Unenthusiastic
23	Repetitious	Resistant	Resentful	Reticent
24	Forgetful	Frank	Fussy	Fearful
25	Interrupts	Impatient	Insecure	Indecisive
26	Unpredictable	Unaffectionate	Unpopular	Uninvolved
27	Haphazard	Headstrong	Hard-to-please	Hesitant
28	Permissive	Proud	Pessimistic	Plain
29	Angered easily	Argumentative	Alienated	Aimless
30	Naive	Nervy	Negative attitude	Nonchalant
31	Wants credit	Workaholic	Withdrawn	Worrier
32	Talkative	Tactless	Too sensitive	Timid
33	Disorganized	Domineering	Depressed	Doubtful
34	Inconsistent	Intolerant	Introvert	Indifferent
35	Messy	Manipulative	Moody	Mumbles
36	Show-off	Stubborn	Skeptical	Slow
37	Loud	Lord-over-others	Loner	Lazy
38	Scatterbrained	Short tempered	Suspicious	Sluggish
39	Restless	Rash	Revengeful	Reluctant
40	Changeable	Crafty	Critical	Compromising
TOTALS				
COMBINED TOTALS				

CPSIA information can be obtained at www.ICGtesting.com
Printed in the USA
LVOW07s1700100114

368920LV00013B/132/P